CONVINCED
BY THE TRUTH

Embracing the Fullness
of Catholic Faith

Modotti Press

AN IMPRINT OF CONNOR COURT PUBLISHING

Published in 2010 by Modotti Press
(an imprint of Connor Court Publishing Pty Ltd)

Modotti Press
PO Box 1,
Ballan VIC 3342
sales@modottipress.com.au
www.modottipress.com.au

Printed in Australia

National Library of Australia
Cataloguing-in-Publication data

Author: Fleming, John I., 1943-

Title: Convinced by the Truth / John I. Fleming.

ISBN: 9781921421112 (pbk.)

Includes bibliographical references and index.

Fleming, John I., 1943-
Catholic Church--Australia--Clergy--Biography.
Priests--Australia--Biography.
Ordination of women.
Lord's Supper--Catholic Church
Lord's Supper--Real presence

Dewey Number: 255.40092

dedicated to my wife Alison, and our three daughters Rebecca, Jane, and Jessica

Table of Contents

Acknowledgements

I am grateful to many people who have assisted me in the writing of a book I thought I would never write. It has taken me many years to get over my reticence in putting into written form an account of the reasons for my decision to become a Catholic. I have chosen to do so now in the wider context of Anglican disintegration, the movement of significant numbers of Anglicans towards the Catholic Church, and the interest shown in Catholicism by so many young people.

My hope is that this book will have a particular appeal to young people. Accordingly I sought and received the generous support of young men and women known to me and who agreed to read the text. They have all provided me with many helpful suggestions. Of course responsibility for the book as a whole is totally mine.

I record here my thanks to Selena Ewing (Southern Cross Bioethics Institute), Rebecca Fleming (my eldest daughter), The Reverend Dr Luke Holohan (Lecturer in Theology at Campion College), Madeleine Meese (Graduate from Campion College), Ruth Russell (former student at Campion College), Robert Simon (family friend), and especially to Peter Zwaans (seminarian in Rome) who made a number of key structural suggestions which greatly improved the presentation of the material. Each of these splendid young men and women made important suggestions for improving the book and I am very grateful to them all.

And special thanks are due to His Grace, Archbishop John Hepworth, Primate of the Traditional Anglican Communion (TAC) who co-authored with me the final chapter of this book which appears as chapter 8. Without his full cooperation and collaboration this vitally important chapter 8 could not have been written, or at least not written in the way that is necessary for telling the full story of the events leading up to the decision of the TAC to apply for full corporate reunion with the Holy See and the subsequent response of the Holy See.

Finally, my wife, Alison, has also contributed to this book not only by being my main supporter through all the difficult times, but also by her gentle encouragement to write it.

This book is dedicated to my wife and three daughters – to Alison, Rebecca, Jane and Jessica.

Preface

The years 2008/2009 were crisis years for members of the Anglican Communion. It is in the process of disintegration because of a range of events which occurred when I was an Anglican, events which influenced me to embrace Catholicism, events which have been cataclysmic for Anglicanism and which are still in the process of being worked out. This book, written in three parts, will help elucidate contemporary events, why things have turned out the way they have for Anglicans. It will also, I believe, give an account of one man's passionate pursuit of the truth no matter what the consequences in the context of the major upheavals in Church and society in the last 40 years, and especially in the last 25 years.

The first part deals with my own personal conversion to Catholicism, and the ordination of women issue which was the catalyst to my conversion.

The first chapter is addressed to my three daughters who were too young at the time to understand or remember the events that eventually led to my conversion and that of my wife to the Catholic Faith in 1987. It is meant to give a full and honest account of my conversion which will be understandable and helpful to a younger generation unencumbered by the social and political assumptions of the generation of 'baby boomers' who seemed to control the agenda twenty years ago. It will provide a modern example of how the truth, once discovered, can be so fundamentally disturbing that it provokes personal crises which in turn can lead to a complete revolution in your family life, your chosen career, and in your social relationships.

In the second chapter I speak of my ordination to the Catholic priesthood in 1995, eight years after having been received into the Church as a layman. I also discuss the question of marriage and priesthood, what it is like to be a married Catholic priest.

The third chapter takes up one of the themes of the first chapter, the ordination of women to the priesthood, and provides a more detailed explanation as to why I found Anglicanism so problematic and the theological arguments advanced by its leaders and opinion-makers lacking in depth, precision, and persuasive power. I was shocked to find Anglican bishops were claiming an authority to do what Christ did not do, even if this meant overturning 2,000 years of Christian fidelity to what Christ did in the matter of ordination to the priesthood, and thereby claiming far greater authority than that actually possessed by the successors of St Peter and the other apostles.

The second part deals with my interaction over the last two years with two young friends, one a Catholic (Mads) and the other not (Robert). They asked me about two key Catholic doctrines concerning the Mass which concerned Robert who was trying to come to grips with the Catholic Faith. Consistent with the first part of the book I try to explain why Catholicism is so intellectually compelling and spiritually satisfying. These chapters will help other young adults who crave the synthesis of faith and reason which only Catholicism can supply, which is why I include them here.

This book had its origins in these chapters with Mads convincing me that I ought to make them more widely available. But the final impetus to write it belongs to my daughters, Rebecca, Jane, and Jessica, and especially Jessica who led me to see that there were so many important things which had affected her parents' story and about which she only had the vaguest memory. My daughters have always been very supportive of my priesthood, and proud to have a priest as their father. But it is as a father that they really know me. I love them all, and am very proud of them. It is fitting that they should have been the ones that, in the end, gave me the motivation to write this book.

It is my hope that others will find these chapters not only coherent, interesting and helpful, but will lead also to them either deepening their knowledge and appreciation of the Catholic Faith or discovering in Catholicism the fullness of the Gospel of Christ, the truth which alone can set us free.

Finally, there are two other chapters in this book. The first, coauthored with Archbishop John Hepworth of the Traditional Anglican Communion (TAC), in a way sums up the logical consequences of the internal contradictions within the Anglican Communion which are playing themselves out at this time. This chapter looks at the anguish of traditional Anglicans who instinctively knew that the Anglican leadership was leading Anglicans well away from what they had always known and understood to be orthodox Biblical Christianity, their desire to find a home in the wider Catholic community, and their developing recognition that the Catholic Church subsists in all those Churches in communion with the Bishop of Rome. Here is traced for the first time the way in which this process was developed, who was involved, how it was implemented, right up to the time when the TAC made its unconditional proposal to Rome in 2007, and Rome's response to that proposal in October 2009. That proposal was the desire of the TAC to be in full communion with the Catholic Church based upon its confession of Catholic Faith as evidenced by the Bishops of the TAC signing a copy of the *Catechism of the Catholic Church*. This historic proposal by the TAC, is the first of its kind since the Reformation, the first time a Reformation ecclesial community has sought reunion with Rome without conditions.

The proposal prompted a response from Rome under the kind and generous leadership of Pope Benedict XVI. On the 20th of October 2009 the Prefect of the Congregation of the Doctrine of the Faith, Cardinal William Lavada, announced that there would soon be "a new provision responding to the many requests from groups of Anglican clergy and faithful in different parts of the world to enter into full visible communion with the Catholic Church". On the 9th of November 2009, the new Apostolic Constitution was made publicly available: Apostolic Constitution Anglicanorum Coetibus Providing for Personal Ordinariates for Anglicans Entering Into full communion With the Catholic Church. Details of this historically unprecedented provision involving members of the Anglican

Communion, a Protestant ecclesial community which arose during the Reformation and separated from Rome, will be discussed in chapter 8.

The second Appendix contains the official text of the Portsmouth Petition to the Holy See.

1
Faith and Conversion –
a father's letter to his daughters

I am writing this letter primarily to you, Rebecca, Jane, and Jessica, my three daughters whom I love so much. When Mum and I left the Anglican Church in which I was an ordained priest and were received into the Catholic Church, you girls were very young, too young to understand what really happened and why. Actually, a lot of other people didn't quite understand it either, and some of those who thought they did, got it wrong. I know that Rebecca has a memory of a lot of these events and so to a lesser extent does Jane. But Jess, you were too young to remember any of them. And talking to you just recently, I came to realise that there were so many gaps in your knowledge of what had happened, I should set it down for you and your sisters. And, in any case, Rebecca and Jane, your remembrance of the events is necessarily at the level of the very young children you were then. The thing is, I have never really explained to you about why I became a Catholic in 1987, the events leading up to it, and the important role your mother played in helping me make my own personal decision. So, I have been persuaded to give a written account of my conversion and, to a lesser extent, that of your mother, because it has become obvious to me that this is something I must do for you.

I am setting it down for you, Rebecca, Jane and Jessica, so that it will also speak to others of your generation who have grown up in a time when 'conversion' is something of a dirty word. In an age of cultural and religious relativism, it is recommended that we should just leave each person to follow his or her own 'truth', whatever that might be. Since there is no "TRUTH", objectively speaking, which could be known, wasn't it arrogant to even think about persuading people to your version of 'truth', just one version among many? And why bother 'converting' if Catholicism is only relatively 'true' and there is no way of telling whether it, or the Anglican account, represents in the fullest sense all that Christ said and did?

So I want to try to explain why, in the end, seeking full communion with the Catholic Church was what I was bound in conscience to do, believing then as I still do that there is objective truth, that truth matters, and that the truth about God matters most. My story is about contemporary issues and has such relevance that it should assist other young people to find many things in it which are helpful to them and their friends. So, in 'fear and trepidation' I am going to tell you about my spiritual odyssey. I say 'fear and trepidation' because there is enough in this account which will reveal a fair bit about my own weakness of will, stupidity, stubborn nature and my self-serving capacity to find reasons why it was better I stayed where I was than make a move. Anyway, here goes!

Teenage years

Let's begin with a little bit about my background. I had a reasonably happy childhood. I was brought up Anglican. My father (your Grandfather whom you never knew) was an Anglican priest (as was my Uncle). Dad had been brought up Methodist, but he became an Anglican under the influence of his brother. He left England for Australia to train for the Anglican ministry and was confirmed by an Anglican bishop on the boat. My mother, an Anglican from birth, became a Catholic when Alison and I did. My father died before you girls were born.

The kind of Anglicanism in which I was brought up in Western Australia was decidedly "middle church C of E" with 'highish' leanings[1]. I was happy enough with that as a kid. After all, I didn't

---

1   The Anglican Church is a Church of compromise between various theological convictions.

know anything else. But as I grew older I found it all rather boring.

When I was 15 the family moved to Adelaide in South Australia, where the style of Anglicanism was decidedly "High". I went to the Billy Graham Crusade and got enthusiastic about religion – for a couple of months. But I was becoming increasingly sceptical about religion in general and belief in God in particular. After all, where was the "proof"?[2] And praying and worshipping all seemed very sterile to me. I didn't "connect" with God and reason was telling me that that was because there was nothing to connect to.

I want it to be clear that I have never accepted the kind of thing that is very fashionable today: "you have your religion, I have mine, you have your truth, I have mine, and there is nothing to say why one 'truth' is better than another. Truth is just a matter of opinion." As I said earlier, this is just nonsense because it simply disproves itself. You can't say there is no truth because in saying that you are asserting a 'truth', ie that there is no truth. In any case, nearly everything we value in the search for answers to our questions is predicated on the belief that there is a truth to be found or we wouldn't bother. Those truths may be philosophical, religious, scientific, or historical. My problem was that I couldn't see a rational justification for belief in God. In fact I thought the proposition that 'God exists' was probably untrue. But even more than that, I would hear people talk about their personal experience of God, an experience which I had never had. I had tried praying but it seemed to me I was just talking to myself!

But, I enjoyed the youth groups and social activities connected with the Church, especially basketball. The "going to Church" bit was tolerable even if not really believable. I didn't particularly like any of the clergy I met finding them fusty, old-fashioned, and not able to speak my language. I am not referring to my father here. He was my Dad, not my priest! That was all before I met Father Brian Ecclestone, a young priest who was the new Chaplain at my school, St Peter's College.

2 For those still puzzled by the strength of arguments for the existence of God, and in the face of the barrage of atheistic books which has recently been published, I recommend two relatively two new books: John Cottingham, *Why Believe?*, London, Continuum, 2009; Anthony Flew, *There is a God: How the World's Most Notorious Atheist Changed His Mind,* New York, Harper One, 2007.

Father Brian was the first priest I could really talk to and he seemed to take an interest in what I had to say even though what I was saying was sceptical, argumentative and without much foundation to it. Looking back it seems that I was not really sure about my lack of belief and so sought him out to see what he would have to say. He challenged me to reconsider the evidence for the resurrection of Jesus which he was able to put to me in a very persuasive way. He was really irritating me because he seemed to be right in the argument he was putting and because he seemed to act consistently with what he taught. I mean he seemed to really care about me and what I thought. I couldn't dislike him (even though I tried to), and I found that what he said about the resurrection and about scepticism in general was undermining my confidence in atheism. You could say I had moved from radical scepticism to being much more open to the possibility of God. But, a belief that God exists, or probably exists, is not the same as belief in God as someone you could actually know and love or who would be remotely interested in human beings. So, I remained unmoved until the age of 18, although more open.

I had a friend whose uncle was the Rector of an Anglican parish in the city, St Mary Magdalene's, Moore Street, Adelaide. He used to brag about how "High Church" his uncle was. So I decided I would check it out. Why not? It might be different from the relatively uninspiring Protestantism I was used to and anyway I was a bit curious. Solemn High Mass in this Church, I think it was on the Feast of the Annunciation of Our Lady in 1962, was a life-changing experience. It was moving, beautiful, absorbing, mysterious and somehow appropriate for the truths it was trying to convey. For the first time I "felt" the presence of God. This service was from the English Missal, what today we would call the Tridentine Mass except that it was in English. And I confess that I found some of the ceremonial amusing, thinking that the servers were searching for sixpenny bits on the floor when all they were doing was saying a Confession. The process of my conversion to belief had now begun but was by no means yet completed.

Around the same time I discovered beautiful liturgical music, the kind that was never heard in my parish church or in my family home. I wandered around Myers and some other stores getting assistants to play me things from different recordings, mostly those made by the Choir of King's College Cambridge. I am speaking of the soaring beauty of polyphonic music, of Palestrina, Byrd, and Vittoria, together with what I could find of Gregorian Chant. Beautiful things, beautiful music, all meant to bring you into touch with God who is the source of all beauty.

All I can say is that at a quite young age, 19, I thought I had discovered that God might be real, and not just as an idea, but as someone who could be known and who might want to know me. Over the next few months conviction grew, and scepticism (although still with me) was tamed. The more I read about Catholic Christianity the more reasonable it all seemed and my intellectual convictions were being matched by my experience in the offering of the Mass. In the end I surrendered and became a Christian by personal conviction, not just upbringing.

But far worse was to come. I was so attracted to the Mass, its music, its tradition and its poetry that I found myself being attracted to the priesthood. I was horrified and tried to push it all away. This was just not meant to happen, not part of my life's plan, such as it was in those days. After a titanic struggle with myself and with God I gave in and went to see the Bishop (Thomas Thornton Reed) and he said, very wisely, I should go to university first, which I did.

Uni was good. In the early 1960s religion was very much a major topic of conversation. That was all to change later when politics and the Vietnam War took over as the hot subjects. But when I was at Uni religious societies ran "missions", the purpose of which was to explain Christianity in a way that would make it attractive to students and even convert them. The Anglican Society and the Student Christian Movement sponsored a mission or two, largely conducted by scarcely believing academics. Then the Humanists ran a counter mission which was always very enjoyable and provoked more heated debates. The Catholics would then bring in the Jesuits for a counter-counter mission, while in later years the Evangelical Union tried its hand in running missions. Through these tumultuous times my Christian Faith and sense of vocation to the priesthood firmed and I believed I was ready for Theological College.

Most importantly, during this time I came to know Christ as a friend, someone upon whom I could rely, someone who loved me unconditionally and could forgive my sins. I had also come to see that faith in God was essential if I was to make any sense out of the world and my place in it. Belief in God was not only reasonable, but safeguarded reason itself. But I notice today an unfortunate trend towards an acceptance of meaninglessness, an impatience with religion because it does not seem to provide an 'instant' fix to life's problems, is not entertaining in the way popular culture is entertaining, and an attitude that religion is only important if it serves my own personal self-interest. But I was now convinced that religion was about putting God first, and if you did that you would find true happiness. Moreover, you have to believe if you wish to understand, and with God you have to believe in Him in order to find Him.

The Writing on the Wall

But, I am overlooking a key event which haunted me for years and finally culminated in my becoming a Catholic. It occurred just after the St Mary Magdalene's experience and before any thought of offering myself for the priesthood. I think it was in 1962.

You see I was friends with a man, Julian Foote, whom I had met on the bus going to school. He was the first real Catholic with whom I had ever had a long conversation. We talked a bit until we got to town when I caught another bus to St Peter's College and he caught his bus to Sacred Heart, Somerton. Anyway, he lived near my place and so I used to visit and fell to arguing with him about religion. He said the Pope was the infallible Head of the Church, Rome was the one true Church, and I was not part of the whole truth. This really irritated me and the truth is, while I was arguing with him I wasn't really listening to what he was saying. I was just arguing to win!

One day he invited me to hear a priest at St Laurence's Catholic Church in North Adelaide who was running an instruction evening for people interested in Catholicism. This particular week he was going to talk about the Pope and would I like to hear him? I don't know why, but I said I would go. My father was very unhappy with me going, but he accepted that he couldn't really stop me.

So, I heard Father Aquinas McComb on the Pope. He began with the Bible and referred to Matthew 16:16-19 which he quoted in full: "And Simon Peter answered and said, Thou art the Christ, the Son of the living God. And Jesus answered and said unto him, Blessed art thou, Simon Barjona: for flesh and blood hath not revealed [it] unto thee, but my Father which is in heaven. And I say also unto thee, *That thou art Peter, and upon this rock I will build my church;* and the gates of hell shall not prevail against it. And I will give unto thee the keys of the kingdom of heaven: and whatsoever thou shalt bind on earth shall be bound in heaven: and whatsoever thou shalt loose on earth shall be loosed in heaven." (Emphasis added)

Now I thought to myself, "Hang on, this guy is misquoting!" I do have a reasonably good memory and I recalled my own father reading that passage in Church and he always said: "on rock *of this kind* I will build my church".

Now Father McComb was arguing on the basis of that passage (and some other ones as well) that the natural meaning of the words was that Peter (which means rock) was the rock on which the Church was built, that he had the 'keys' or authority to run the Church in the absence, so to speak, of Jesus, and that he was therefore the touchstone of unity within the Church. But my father's version was "on rock of this kind". I was confused, argued a bit with Father McComb, but had a sinking feeling he was right. And when I went home and got out the Book of Common Prayer and looked up the Gospel reading for St Peter's Day I saw with my own eyes that he was quoting truly. My father was actually falsifying the text as he read it, no doubt because he wanted to put his own spin on it.

Did that mean I should rush off and join the Catholic Church? No. While I was tempted to do just that, I just felt I couldn't do it. Nor did I want to because I was happy as an Anglo-Catholic. I persuaded myself that I was both too young and ignorant to make that independent decision, that I had to honour my father and mother which meant not rejecting Anglicanism.

However, the incident was deeply unsettling and the impression it made on me lasted for a long time, gradually fading, but never really leaving me. My compromise, for that indeed was what it was, was to accept all the Catholic teachings, or at least the ones I knew then, and do my best to be as Catholic as possible but without the Pope. That is, I was a convinced Anglo-Catholic.

Of course I was being completely illogical wasn't I? It was the argument about the papacy that convinced me of the truth of Catholicism, so I accepted Catholicism but not the papacy which was an integral part of Catholicism. Not smart. But that's where I was then.

Julian left school and joined the Dominicans. He is now Father Laurence Foote OP. Me? I left school, went to University, got radicalised in left wing politics, but still somehow stuck with Christianity, confused and all as I was about it and its teachings, especially its moral teachings. They say if you can remember the 1960s you weren't really there. Well I do and I was!

Theological College

In 1967 I eventually went to St Barnabas' Theological College in Belair. My education in theology could now begin. It was very heavily Biblical for which I am very grateful. The winds of 'modernism' were blowing strongly. Theologians were speculating on the 'death of God', that 'man had come of age and could stand up and eyeball God without having to cringe because of an overwhelming sense of unworthiness', and that we could begin to think of Jesus less as God and more as a man like us. My theology lecturer was besotted with Paul Tillich, Rudolph Bultmann, John MacQuarrie and other 'existentialist' theologians. He certainly didn't like my preoccupation with the Church Fathers, let alone old-fashioned obscurantists like St Thomas Aquinas and his (then) modern day apologists such as the Anglican priest-theologian Eric Mascall. I wasn't bothered by this because I was arrogant enough to think that I could do this Catholic thing on my own and that everyone else would or could be persuaded by my brilliant account of it. Given time they would all come to see and accept the truth.

You see, I wanted to remain Catholic but still in the Anglican Church. While I was intellectually convinced by the Catholic Faith, the fact is that personally, culturally, and emotionally I was an Anglican. There were great Anglican Catholic intellectuals under whose influence I came, especially Eric Mascall and John Henry Newman. Mascall, priest and philosopher-theologian, was a follower and interpreter of the great Roman Catholic theologian St Thomas Aquinas. I read his books avidly and became even further convinced of the Anglo-Catholic account.

Where Newman was concerned I believe I deliberately avoided reading his books directly, instead taking on many of his ideas through the writings of others. He had become a Catholic and I was subconsciously concerned about the effect he might have on me. Newman had been one of the originators of a movement in the Church of England called the Oxford Movement. This movement, emanating from the University of Oxford, was an attempt to reclaim the 'Catholicity' of the Church of England and represented a revolt against the State running the affairs of the Church.

Newman and others wrote a number of short articles or 'tracts' setting out their position on various matters they considered to be very important, pamphlets to challenge religious positions taken for granted in Protestant England. These 'tracts' were very controversial but none as controversial as the last of them, 'Tract 90'. But it was Tract 90 that I loved best.

In this famous Tract 90 (25 January 1841) Newman wrote an essay which explored ways in which he could reconcile the teachings of the Anglican Church found in the Book of Common Prayer (1662) and the 39 Articles of religion with the dogmatic teachings of the Roman Catholic Council of Trent[3] which had been convened by the Pope

---

3 "The nineteenth ecumenical council opened at Trent on 13 December, 1545, and closed there on 4 December, 1563. Its main object was the definitive determination of the doctrines of the Church in answer to the heresies of the Protestants; a further object was the execution of a thorough reform of the inner life of the Church by removing the numerous abuses that had developed in it." Cf Catholic Encyclopedia website http://www.newadvent.org/cathen/15030c.htm.

to deal with 'Protestant errors'. Tract 90 caused an enormous public uproar in England and was universally condemned by the bishops of the Church of England. This was the last straw for Newman who retired to the tiny village of Littlemore before being eventually received into the Catholic Church by Father (now Blessed) Dominic Barbieri in October 1845. Many, many years later Newman explained his conversion in a series of articles which were finally published in a single volume, *Apologia Pro Vita Sua*. It was always suggested to me that the *Apologia* was too subversive a book for a young man who was already showing to his closest friends all the symptoms of a terminal bout of 'Roman fever'.

What I am saying here is that although I was being schooled in 'liberal Anglo-Catholicism' by my teachers, I was actually far more impressed and persuaded by orthodox Catholicism. But I persuaded myself that you could be just as good a Catholic without the Pope, just like the Orthodox. After all weren't Anglican Orders valid? Didn't I have the sacraments? And the undoubted convenience of this position is that it would allow me to stay in the Church of my own cultural origins. Did I like the Englishness of Anglicanism? Absolutely! I loved it.

Mass Media and controversy loom

On the 2 February 1970 (the Feast of the Purification of the Blessed Virgin Mary), I was ordained a priest in the Anglican Church in the Diocese of Adelaide, South Australia. It was just the most wonderful time for me. My first Mass was great and I was beginning a whole new life – still beset with doubts about Anglicanism but reading everything I could to keep me both Anglican and, as I thought, Catholic.

In June of that year I was asked to debate 'censorship' with Eric Williams from the Workers Education Association (WEA) on Radio 5AD, an Adelaide radio commercial station. A 5AD personality, Keith Conlon, who was and remains a good friend, suggested my name to an on-air colleague as someone who could debate a bit. It was a good close debate and I enjoyed it. A few days later 5DN got in touch with me to audition for them. 5AD heard about it and made me an offer to do a morning programme five days a week. 34 years later and I was still doing radio. In addition I wrote weekly columns for the *Adelaide Advertiser* for about 13 years. But I loved radio best of all and it seemed to suit me. Actually, I really miss it now but that's what happens when you shift from Adelaide to Sydney and you are already 61!

Access to the media gave me ample opportunity to flaunt my ego and also to bring some influence to bear on public debates. You really can't do radio unless you have a big ego, an ego which needs to be tamed and directed to a good end. Many of these debates were on bioethical issues such as abortion, euthanasia, and embryonic stem cell technology. Others touched on more general issues such as family, marriage, divorce, sport, politics, local chit chat and even the idea that Australia would abandon its Monarchy for some unspecified experiment in republicanism.

But real controversy erupted around me when, in 1976, I wrote a very short piece on 'women priests' for the *Advertiser* explaining the Church's traditional position. An exchange with Archbishop Keith Rayner, my Anglican Archbishop, followed. His attitude deeply disturbed and puzzled me. I knew that Anglicans had discussed women's ordination at the 1968 Lambeth Conference but I hadn't realised how serious the situation really was.

You see, I had been brought up to believe bishops were defenders of the Catholic Faith and it never occurred to me that bishops would be revolutionaries, undermining the Faith as it had been received, and thereby claiming an authority which even the Pope did not claim.

In the previous year your mother and I married. I will go into that episode a little later in this book, but for the moment all that needs to be noted is that we married on the 4 January 1975.

England – 'the demi-paradise'

At about this time your mother and I decided that the time was right for us to go to England, partly to get away from Adelaide, partly for Alison to return to the country of her birth and upbringing, and partly to allow me to engage with my own British roots. We needed to get away from Adelaide because we were not long married, I was very well known in Adelaide through my media work, and we both thought it would be good if your mother and I could share our first years of marriage away from a situation where she was known as "Father John's wife". It enabled us to start our marriage on a more equal footing and gave me breathing space from local theological controversies.

I was appointed Assistant Curate in the Parish of St Nicholas, Chiswick, in West London. I had always been attracted to England, partly because it was the tradition of my father, and my mother on her father's side, and partly because Alison was born and brought up in the UK. It was a good time for your mother and me to be away from Australia. I loved England and felt at home there, spiritually, socially, and culturally. How did Shakespeare describe England? He thought of it as:

> This royal throne of kings, this sceptred isle,
> This earth of majesty, this seat of Mars,
> This other Eden, demi-paradise,
> This fortress built by Nature for herself
> Against infection and the hand of war,
> This happy breed of men, this little world,
> This precious stone set in the silver sea,
> Which serves it in the office of a wall
> Or as a moat defensive to a house,
> Against the envy of less happier lands, –
> This blessed plot, this earth, this realm, this England.[4]

I fell in love with England, its cathedrals and mediaeval churches. It was as though in a way I was in Catholic England, the true home of Anglicanism where all my doubts about Anglicanism could be put to rest, finally. Was not the Church of England a branch of the Catholic Church together with the Eastern Orthodox Churches?

---

4 William Shakespeare (1564 - 1616), "King Richard II", Act 2 scene 1.

Could you not 'feel' the Sarum[5] tradition all around you? Were not Roman Catholics just the "Italian Mission to England" and the "Irish Catholic Mission" – culturally foreign and just not English. St Nicholas' Church in Chiswick (a parish in West London), where I served as a Curate, had a wonderful Anglo-Catholic Priest as Vicar, Father Patrick Tuft. He, and his wife Pauline, remain our good friends to this day, as do Martin and Diane Daly from the same parish.

Throughout most of my time at Chiswick I carried on as if there was no crisis for me. I was happy to be in 'Catholic' England, and without too much concern about the storm clouds of extreme Anglican liberalism which were gathering around and above us. The truth is that I allowed myself, willed myself, to be beguiled by an English culture which seemed to suggest, or at the least be consistent with, Catholicism but which, in reality, was a Protestant conceit.[6] I just did not want to face up to the 'signs of the times' which were portents of a powerful storm about to deluge us with the great Anglican compromise between Christianity and state sponsored secularism.

For example, a number of 'theologians' from the Anglican and Protestant traditions put together a book called *The Myth of God Incarnate*. The point of the book was to cast doubt on the idea that Jesus is fully God and fully man. Fully God and fully man He certainly was and is, according to orthodox Catholic teaching. But this fundamental doctrine was openly under sustained attack from Protestantism's 'brightest and best' and without a single Anglican bishop uttering a word of protest.

Well, I went to see the Bishop of Kensington, a Suffragan bishop in London to whom I was responsible, a good chap really. His name was Ronnie Goodchild. He explained to me that the Church of England was a big place (alongside the Catholic Church and the Orthodox Churches the Church of England is, in fact, actually very small fry indeed), and that there was room for everyone and for

---

5 Sarum refers to the liturgy of Salisbury, the dominant way in which the Mass was celebrated in England prior to the Reformation.

6 Helen Gardner says that "a conceit is a comparison whose ingenuity is more striking than its justness". Helen Gardner, *The Metaphysical Poets* (Oxford University Press), 1961, "Introduction" p. xxiii.

the widest range of views, including, apparently, frankly heretical
views.

Later, one of the contributors to that book, Don Cupitt, a
particularly brilliant philosopher, wrote a new book called *Taking Leave
of God*, which prompted the historian David Edwards to opine that
he rather thought Cupitt had "taken leave of his senses".

Why do I refer to this? Well it is my way of suggesting that
even given the mediaeval Catholic trappings which still clung to the
institution itself, like barnacles to an abandoned ship, the Church of
England looked increasingly like a perpetual debating competition
with no adjudicator. Or, put another way, a game of football without
an umpire, each playing according to his own rules. But in all honesty I
have to admit I was prepared to tolerate the intolerable so that I could
remain in the Church of England, persuading myself that the Church
of England was really a Catholic Church with some Protestants in it
and a small minority of heretics in high places, when in fact it was a
Protestant Church with some Catholics in it.

Nor did I really want to face up to the Erastianism[7] of the Church
of England. At the Reformation the state (i.e. the King) nationalised
religion making it subject to the definitive whims of the King. The
Church gave the King legitimacy through the Coronation, and the
King gave the Church a favoured social and political position subject,
of course, to the bishops of the Church making their obeisance to the
King. The longer I lived in the Church of England the more bizarre
such an arrangement seemed to me and the more uncomfortable I
felt about it. Still, this was what I inherited and maybe everything
would be 'fixed' when the Church of England was reunited with
Rome. Anyhow, the rest of the Anglican Communion was made up
of non-Erastian Anglican Churches who were in full communion with
each other. That is, Erastianism was not, or so I persuaded myself,
essential to Anglican belief. It might even be helpful in keeping the
Church of England faithful to the doctrine of the Book of Common
Prayer and the 39 Articles of Religion.

Just before returning to Australia in 1978 Alison and I went to

---

7 The subordination of the authority of the Church to the authority of the State.

the Lambeth Conference[8] where we worked in the Media Centre. We saw many things, including the team of spies from Idi Amin's Uganda who, masquerading as press corps, kept their eyes on the Ugandan bishops to make sure they didn't spill the beans about what was really going on in Uganda. We also saw the extravagances of the American Episcopal bishops whose preoccupation with episcopal sartorial elegance (i.e. the latest fashions in bishops' clothes and jewellery) was only matched by their arrogance, especially where so-called Third World bishops were concerned. They just knew they were right about women priests, homosexuality and the like and the black bishops, (whose simplicity of life, saintliness and zeal for the Faith put them to shame), were comparatively ignorant and uneducated, without the benefit of the Western Enlightenment; to be funded and tolerated provided they didn't complain too much. The storm clouds of a fundamental crisis in Anglicanism were gathering and I was feeling very insecure because I could sense that the very things which kept me Anglican, a valid priesthood and valid sacraments, were now under serious threat.

During this Lambeth Conference of 1978 I had the good fortune to meet my spiritual 'twin', Father Peter Geldard, the newly appointed General Secretary of the English Church Union. At a pub in Canterbury one night we met to talk about everything to do with the Anglican Church and the Catholic Faith. It was a bit 'spooky' really as we seemed to agree on literally everything, discovering similarities in our political pasts, and even expressing ourselves using the same expressions and metaphors. Alison sat there gobsmacked as she listened to two arrogant Anglican priests impressing each other with their wisdom, insight, and agreement!

The English Church Union, at that time a moribund religious and political organisation, was revivified under Geldard's leadership and

---

8 The Lambeth Conference is a meeting of the bishops of the Anglican Communion from all over the world held every ten years. The Archbishop of Canterbury's London home is Lambeth Palace where the first Lambeth conferences were held. Eventually the numbers were too big for a meeting to be held there. In 1978, the meeting was held at the University of Kent in Canterbury, overlooking Canterbury Cathedral. The local Catholics mischievously refer to the beautiful Cathedral as "the shack"!

became once again the flagship activist Anglo-Catholic organisation. The Church Union under Father Geldard took up the fight in the General Synod of the Church of England for, among many other things, the retention of the male-only priesthood not only because it was right but in order to maintain the possibility of the reunion of the Church of England with the Catholic Church. He, like me, was an Anglo-Papalist, that impossibly illogical Anglican view which held that while we could have Catholicism without the Pope, in fact we really believed in the Papacy as essential to the reunified Church and personally preferred to accept the Pope's authoritative pronouncements in everything except becoming a Catholic in fact!

We became friends, really good friends. He was, and is, one in whom I could confide my doubts and fears about Anglicanism. I invited him to Australia often to speak to Anglo-Catholics and keep them enthused about the prospects of reunion with Rome and the need to keep the Anglican Church in such a condition that reunion was really possible. He is a brilliant orator and could always be relied on to come to conferences and other events and to be a great encourager of his fellow Anglo-Catholic priests as well as the laity. On one occasion he was with us in time to be Godfather for Jessica at her Baptism. He was always such a good friend and ally, and in the dangerous waters I was then treading I certainly needed good priestly friends.

Anyway, Geldard and I were at this special meeting with Anglo-Catholic bishops at the Lambeth Conference where it was decided that we would all embark on a process of Catholic renewal in the Anglican Church in the country from which we came. I agreed to lead the charge in Australia with Bishop John Hazelwood of Ballarat supporting me. But when I returned to Australia and travelled to Ballarat to see him and begin the planning I soon discovered that he, Bishop Hazelwood[9], had lost interest, if indeed he ever had it. I had to find other more reliable allies. To achieve this I, in company with others, set up the Union of Anglican Catholic Priests, a Union committed to keeping the Anglican Church Catholic.

Return to Australia

Alison and I returned to Australia in 1978, and I took up an appointment at the Church of the Good Shepherd, Plympton, in the Diocese of Adelaide. I loved that parish and the people in it. It grew substantially in the time I was there and life was good. Alison and I started a family with Rebecca being born in December 1980, Jane in 1982, and Jessica in 1985. I loved being a father and I had always hoped we would have daughters because my family was Mum, Dad, five boys and only one sister, Wendy, who was six years older than me.

But these years also turned out to be some of the most turbulent in my life. It all began well enough as I co-wrote two books with my great friend Daniel Ch Overduin, a Lutheran pastor and theologian. I was enjoying academic life again, albeit on a part-time basis, and had begun to read 'subversive books' (more of that later). In addition I was deeply involved in Catholic renewal within the Anglican Church of Australia with the single purpose of aiding what I saw as the great moment in history, the realisation of the goal of full communion between the Anglican Church and the Catholic Church.

Did I really believe that could happen? I certainly did and here are the reasons why.

The 1960s was a time of optimism about the future, about the possibility of peace not only in Europe but also between the

---

9 Hazelwood was one of the most unreliable men I ever met. I recall a sermon he preached in which he referred to himself as "Peter", claiming the powers of St Peter. I saw him vote for women's ordination at the General Synod of 1985, and also fulminate against such ordinations. Finally, he again capitulated in favour of women's ordination for the sake of what he called 'unity' which he rated more highly than anything else. By 'unity' he didn't have anything ecumenical in mind he was just concerned about his "friends from Melbourne down the Highway". Cf Muriel Porter, *Women in the Church – The Great Ordination Debate In Australia*, Ringwood Victoria, Penguin Books, 1989, 152.

Churches, members of which had fought together in the trenches against what seemed like the overwhelming power of atheism as incarnated in Nazism and Communism. If the Churches couldn't get it together who could?

The Anglican Church made a number of tentative approaches to Rome which, on the 24 March 1966, culminated in the Common Declaration of Pope Paul VI and Dr Michael Ramsey, Archbishop of Canterbury. This Declaration contained a commitment to enter into a 'serious dialogue' in an attempt to remove all such serious obstacles that would 'stand in the way of a restoration of complete communion of faith and sacramental life'.[10] At the Lambeth Conference of 1968 this initiative by the Pope and the Archbishop of Canterbury was fully supported with the Lambeth Fathers recommending the 'setting up of a Permanent Joint Commission … This commission or its sub-commissions should consider the question of inter-communion in the context of a true sharing in faith and the mutual recognition of ministry …'[11]

Now I believed the Anglicans were really, really serious in their intentions and I had no reason to doubt the word of the Pope. The reason why I was so convinced of good Anglican intentions was because the Anglican zeal for unity had been expressed in the previous Lambeth Conferences of 1908, 1920, and 1930. In fact the Committee of Bishops working on 'Renewal In Unity' in 1968 recalled the 1908 statement and its reiteration at the two subsequent Lambeth Conferences in these terms:

> There can be no fulfillment of the Divine purpose in any scheme of reunion which does not ultimately include the great Latin Church of the West, with which our history has been so closely associated in the past, and to which we are still bound by so many close ties of common faith and tradition.[12]

---

10 *The Final Report of ARCIC*, SPCK London 1982, 118 and cf John Fleming, "To The Intent That These Orders May Be Continued …", in David Wetherell ed., *Women Priests in Australia? The Anglican Crisis.* Melbourne. Spectrum.1987, 97.
11 'Renewal In Unity' in *The Lambeth Conference 1968 Resolutions And Reports,* SPCK London, 1986, 136.
12 *Ibid.,* 138.

If you add to all this the intentions of Pope Paul VI and Archbishop Ramsey in the Common Declaration of 1966 and the terms of reference set out in it, one can easily see why unity was thought to be so close, so achievable, and something to which one could commit oneself. Their intentions were

> to inaugurate between the Roman Catholic Church and the Anglican Communion a serious dialogue which, *founded on the Gospels and the ancient common traditions,* may lead to that unity in truth, for which Christ prayed.[13] [Emphasis added]

One of the ancient common traditions between the two churches was, of course, the Apostolic Ministry of Bishops, Priests, and Deacons. Within eight years of the Lambeth Conference of 1968 agreeing to the terms of the Dialogue, the Protestant Episcopal Church of the USA (PECUSA) and the Anglican Church in Canada, followed closely by the Anglican Church in New Zealand, had shamelessly dishonoured their own word and unilaterally changed one of the ancient common traditions. Even worse, they did so without consulting other parts of the Anglican Communion or the Catholic Church.

Moreover, as I later discovered, Donald Coggan, Archbishop of Canterbury, had previously written to the Pope in July 1975 requesting "ecumenical counsel" regarding an alleged emerging consensus among Anglicans that there appeared to be no fundamental objections to the ordination of women to the priesthood. You don't ask for "counsel" unless you are prepared to listen to it. On the 30th November 1975 the Pope replied that the Catholic Church held that "it is not admissible to ordain women to the priesthood, for very fundamental reasons." In other words, with all due respect to the Anglican opinion-makers, there were, in fact, fundamental objections, fundamental reasons why women could not be ordained to the priesthood. The Pope identified these reasons as:

- The example of Christ who chose only men as apostles (Scripture).

---

13 *The Final report of ARCIC,* 118.

- The Church's constant imitation of the example of Christ (Tradition).
- And the Church's consistent teaching that this practice is "in accordance with God's plan for his Church" (Magisterium).[14]

The implication here is that, at this stage, the Archbishop of Canterbury was acting honourably in consulting his partner in the ecumenical cause. All of this had no impact on PECUSA, the Canadians and the New Zealanders who were prepared to dishonour the commitment they had previously made to the ecumenical project. Within 12 months they had effectively dismissed the "ecumenical counsel" that the Archbishop of Canterbury had asked for and received. It was surely not rocket science to see that the Pope's clear and straightforward answer was a serious signal to the Anglicans that such a development would signal serious ecumenical problems for the future.

I remember visiting the Council for Christian Unity in Rome with Father Geldard in 1981, and talking to the late Monsignor Richard Purdy. He described the ecumenical process with the Anglicans in terms of being on a roller coaster, coming down the hill with the finishing line now in sight, when suddenly a large piece of concrete appeared in the middle of the road. He described how disappointed he was that there had been no consultation with their partners in dialogue, simply a letter from the Episcopalians saying that they had unilaterally ordained women. To put it mildly, I was very surprised to learn of this discourtesy and very angry indeed that the Anglican Communion, within eight years of giving its word to the Holy See, had effectively dishonoured its own freely entered into ecumenical obligations.

---

14 Details of this may be found in "Letters Exchanged by Pope and Anglican Leader", Origins 6:9 (12 August 1976): 129.131-132. It should be noted here that the Pope supplies the "reasons" but not at this stage the evidence and arguments in support of these reasons which were not to appear until the publication of Inter Insigniores in 1976.

The Ordination of Women debate in Australia

By now I was becoming even more seriously disturbed about the nature of the Anglican Church and my continuing membership of it. However, always the optimist, and wanting to remain an Anglican for reasons now more of convenience than conviction, I thought the battle could still be won to keep the Anglican Church Catholic, or at least Catholic enough to maintain a serious dialogue with Rome. Even if we lost the Americans (only four million in that Church anyway and many of them very unhappy with their Church's decision), we could still keep the Anglican Communion on course provided the Church of England and the Nigerian Church remained faithful to the Catholic and Apostolic Ministry. After all, together they comprised about 53 million of the 70 million members of the Anglican Communion.

But even though in my heart of hearts I knew that the fight would be a political fight and that the pro-ordination of women lobby would never take "no" for an answer, I decided to fight on for what I thought was my heritage. And what was that? To be an English Christian, following the English Catholic tradition, safeguarded in a Church which was, in essence, Catholic. Well, we didn't have the Pope, but all the signs were there that reunification was just around the corner if people would just keep their sights on that goal and not be sidetracked by other issues. In any case I felt completely at home and comfortable within Ecclesia Anglicana.[15] Yes, I had to fight hard to convince other Anglicans that they were really Catholic but not 'Roman", and so belonged to a branch of the one true Church. But I had become used to that.

The thought of uprooting myself from all I knew, all I had ever known, was too disturbing for me to seriously contemplate. Reason would prevail, would it not? So why then was I having all these doubts? Why did I keep feeling so uncomfortable within my own comfort zone? It just didn't make any sense. And what was Alison thinking? We talked about the issue but without really talking about what we would 'do', skirting around the conversion issue as if it didn't really exist. She, like me, was against the ordination of women and for the same reasons.

---

15 The technical Latin name for the Anglican Church.

But, Rebecca, Jane and Jess, there was more to the story, particularly affecting me, your father, which sharpened the issues for me. I shall now recount the events which led me away from Anglicanism and ultimately into the Church of Rome.

Intellectual conversion

In the early 1980s I found myself generously invited into the Melbourne Catholic intellectual community by outstanding people like Father Frank Harman, Dr Nicholas Tonti-Filippini, Father Tom Daly SJ, and Dr Joe Santamaria. Through these people and others I discovered the whole natural law tradition and the fascinating discussions that were ongoing in the postconciliar period. Under these influences a decisive intellectual conversion was begun without my being really aware of it. I am deeply grateful to these people and many other Catholic intellectuals who have been so open, generous, and personally influential. Among these other intellectuals were people I was reading and had never at that time met personally.

For example, in 1983 Joe Santamaria and Nick Tonti-Filippini made sure that I bought a copy of Germain Grisez's *The Way of the Lord Jesus Volume 1*. At about the same time I acquired John Finnis's *Natural Law and Natural Rights*, and soon after his *Fundamentals of Ethics*. All three volumes were to have a profound effect on my intellectual development and understanding of the Catholic moral tradition. At about the same time I became acquainted with the works of William E May and also those of an opposing school of thought, the proportionalists, such as Charles Curran and Richard McCormick, not to mention Richard McBrien. That is, I was reading both sides to one of the great and protracted debates in moral theology of the late twentieth century.

Not only did I find myself thrust into the great debate between proportionalists and traditional natural law theorists, I became aware of the new approaches to natural law theory as epitomised by Germaine Grisez, John Finnis, Joseph Boyle, and defended by May and Shaw.

For the first time I was being given a really good insight into

Aristotle and Aquinas, and a philosophical framework within which I could make sense of Catholic moral teaching. In the Anglican Church I had been left to fend for myself, trying to make sense of New Testament ethics and such a reading of St Thomas Aquinas as I could manage on my own, and seeing how they could be applied to contemporary ethical issues.

The point here is that for the first time I was developing a consistent and intellectually rigorous approach to moral questions, and especially to those questions that had always challenged me. Those issues concerned sexual morality, contraception, and human rights. But I was always challenged as to how I could defend the Christian moral tradition on its merits, so to speak, without exclusive appeal to the data of Revelation. I was opposed to abortion on the obvious moral grounds of the wrongfulness of killing innocent human beings and, from my scientific background, the even more obvious fact that the unborn were human beings just like the rest of us. I was confused on the moral questions because my Protestant background gave me no intellectual basis upon which I could systematically deal with the moral questions that faced contemporary society and which so deeply interested and concerned me.

In many ways I owe Finnis, Grisez, Boyle, and May more than I could ever adequately express. In company with the Melbourne Catholic intellectuals, they gave me the insight into Catholicism that I so much needed. The timing was, in terms of God's plan for me, perfect and in many ways made my conversion to the Catholic Church inescapable if I was to be intellectually honest.

The Great Crunch Time

In 1985 I attended the General Synod of the Anglican Church of Australia as a priest duly elected by the Synod of the Archdiocese of Adelaide to represent that Archdiocese. Peter Carnley, Archbishop of Perth, and David Penman, Archbishop of Melbourne, introduced a canon (law) to permit the ordination of women. Carnley led the charge and in his speech asked, rhetorically, whether the ordination of women was within the limits of 'tolerable plurality' within the

Anglican Church. What Carnley didn't know was that I had been asked by Archbishop Donald Robinson of Sydney to lead the opposition and was thus given opportunity for a thirty minute reply. I argued that the simple answer to the Carnley rhetoric was "No".

An accurate review of my opposition is to be found in Muriel Porter's book, in which I am described as a priest with "a high media profile", "a skilled communicator" and whose barbs were 'sharp'. A lot of what I said is rehearsed in this chapter. Porter also reported that "at the General Synod, rumours were circulating that Fleming would become a Roman Catholic if women were ordained priests in Australia. He subsequently made that change a few months before the 1987 Special General Synod. Now a Catholic layman, his voice is no longer heard in Anglican circles."[16] What Porter did not know, and could not have known, was that the die had already been cast and not because of women's ordination but because of underlying questions to which the women's ordination issue inexorably led.

In the quietness of my home I had already asked myself this fundamental question in light of all of the reading which I had done and all of the things I had been forced to confront. That question was this: I am just one Anglican priest, not a theologian, or at least no more so than most of the most prominent advocates for women's ordination. I could be quite wrong about women's ordination. If I am wrong, from whom would I take correction? The Anglican Church? Absolutely not! Then from whom? I answered, "The Pope and the Catholic Church". The absurdity of this answer struck me with great force. I would not take correction from the Church to which I did belong, but I would take correction from the Church to which I did not belong. This was because the Pope was the infallible head of the Church, and the Anglican Church was no real Church with real authority but a free association of Christians with Ministers of doubtful validity.

This answer was deeply shocking to me as I had invested my life in what I thought was a branch of the Catholic Church with priests

16 Muriel Porter, *Women in the Church: The Great Ordination Debate in Australia*, Ringwood, Victoria, Australia, 1989, 113-114.

who were real priests. Subsequently I read the fatal book, John Henry Newman's *Apologia Pro Vita Sua*, a book I had never read before probably out of fear as to what I might find in it. Newman destroyed any last vestiges of Anglicanism in me. I found the 'paper theory' of the branch Church destroyed by the very man who had so eloquently promoted it. Tract 90 was a charade, disavowed by its own author soon after he had published it. What on earth was I to do?

The Pope, Authority, and Conscience

Now, girls, here's the thing: all these years since 1962, that encounter with Father McComb to which I referred earlier in this chapter, never left me. "You are Peter and on this Rock I will build my Church." All that I had subsequently read, *Lumen Gentium*, John Tillard's *The Bishop of Rome*, and a myriad of text books too many to detail here, were all pushing me to the same conclusion about the Petrine Office, the nature and constitution of the Church, the unity of the Church and what is essential to Catholicity. What had happened, little by little, so gradually that I cannot pin down the exact time when it occurred, was that I had internalised Catholic doctrine and made it my own. I was a Catholic believer in the fullest sense, and despite heroic attempts to remain Anglican. The ordination of women debate had been the catalyst for a complete rethinking of my own theological positions and the conclusions I reached devastated me. I had been broken and remade, not in a dramatic moment of inspiration, but gradually, imperceptibly, and in the end decisively.

Even worse, I had for some years been reading – devouring – the documents of the Second Vatican Council. In *Dignitatis Humanae* I found these very troubling passages:

> It is in accordance with their dignity as persons – that is, beings endowed with reason and free will and therefore privileged to bear personal responsibility – that all men should be at once impelled by nature and also bound by a moral obligation to seek the truth, especially religious truth. They are also bound to adhere to the truth, once it is known, and to order their whole lives in accord with

the demands of truth.[17] [n 2]

On his part, man perceives and acknowledges the imperatives of the divine law through the mediation of conscience. In all his activity a man is bound to follow his conscience in order that he may come to God, the end and purpose of life. It follows that he is not to be forced to act in manner contrary to his conscience. Nor, on the other hand, is he to be restrained from acting in accordance with his conscience, especially in matters religious. The reason is that the exercise of religion, of its very nature, consists before all else in those internal, voluntary and free acts whereby man sets the course of his life directly toward God. No merely human power can either command or prohibit acts of this kind.(3) The social nature of man, however, itself requires that he should give external expression to his internal acts of religion: that he should share with others in matters religious; that he should profess his religion in community. Injury therefore is done to the human person and to the very order established by God for human life, if the free exercise of religion is denied in society, provided just public order is observed.[18] [n 3]

If I was to take religious truth really seriously then I could no longer in good conscience continue as an Anglican, let alone as an Anglican priest. The die was cast.

Time to make the plunge

Two days before you, Jess, were to be born, I went to lunch with Monsignor Robert Aitken, Vicar General of the Catholic Archdiocese of Adelaide, to see whether he would be receptive to my desire to become a Catholic. You see, girls, I had made tentative inquiries before about becoming a Catholic, but had been turned away. I was told by a

---

17 Declaration on Religious Freedom, *Dignitatis Humanae*, Promulgated by His Holiness Pope Paul VI, 7 December 1965, n 2.
18 *Ibid.*, n. 3.

priest that I should not be considering these things because Rome had moved past "individual conversions" and that it would be better to "stay where you are and assist the ecumenical process". Foolishly I had accepted this advice. But now, I could do so no longer. I simply did not want to introduce anyone else into the Anglican Church because I no longer believed that it was truly a Catholic Church. And in any case, this was all about the truth, conscience, and my obligation to take what I knew was the only logical step. "In all his activity a man is bound to follow his conscience in order that he may come to God, the end and purpose of life. It follows that he is not to be forced to act in manner contrary to his conscience."[19]

Looking back I am still surprised and even scandalised that I should have been given advice against the clear teaching of the Fathers of the Second Vatican Council, "that all men should be at once impelled by nature and also bound by a moral obligation to seek the truth, especially religious truth. They are also bound to adhere to the truth, once it is known, and to order their whole lives in accord with the demands of truth."[20]

But it was really silly of me to have listened to that advice and for at least two years to have followed it. What that priest said was unfortunate and I believe he was well-intentioned. But the real fault is mine and mine alone. I was far too weak in my resolve, and too inclined to accept advice which would seem to justify me staying in my own comfort zone. I think, but I cannot now be absolutely sure of it, that I found some comfort in that advice, that it would relieve me of the need to completely disrupt my life, and offered me an 'easy' way out while still providing a balm to my interior conscientious doubts and fears about Anglicanism. I was being offered a 'soft option', and was probably grateful to embrace that option because it meant I didn't have to 'do' anything.

Well if I did think that advice would give me comfort I was really badly mistaken.

Fortunately for me, though, on my second and more serious

---

19 *Ibid.*
20 *Ibid.*, n. 2.

attempt to become a Catholic, I had come to the right priest at the right time. Father Aitken went above and beyond the call of duty to see me, Alison, and yes, even my own mother, safely received into full communion with the Catholic Church. Even then he was subject to criticism not only for doing this, but also because he received us into the Church the day after I announced my resignation from Anglicanism. But he had kept Archbishop Faulkner fully informed throughout the process and acted with the Archbishop's full approval.

During the two years which elapsed between that first meeting with Monsignor Aitken and taking the final step I really struggled. I saw Fr Aitken regularly and I was still reading, trying to find reasons why I did not and perhaps even should not leave the Anglican Church; all to no avail. The more I read the more convinced I was that I had to make the change. Saying Mass in the Anglican rite became ever more difficult and I was beset with concerns about the validity of Anglican Orders, and the efficacy of Anglican rites.

Then, like a bolt out of the blue, Alison, your mother, informed me that she, at any rate, had made her decision and that decision was to become a Catholic. She had become completely disillusioned with Anglican bishops claiming an authority to change the faith of the Church unilaterally. She said she would wait for me as long as she could. In many ways this was a relief because I could see no other way for me than Rome, it being more a question now of how and when rather than if. When Pope John Paul II visited Adelaide in 1986 she took you girls to the Papal Mass. Where was I? Celebrating an Anglican Mass in the Plympton parish church of which I was the Rector. Where did I really want to be?

Traumas, troubles and Providence

Your mother was pregnant with you, Jess, when I began what turned out to be the two year process to disengage from Anglicanism and be received into the full communion with the Catholic Church. And when we finally left in 1987 Rebecca, you were six, Jane you were four, and Jess you were only 19 months old. It is all very well for a

43-year-old Anglican priest deciding he wants to become a Catholic even given that his wife is breaking her neck, so to speak, to get into the Church as well. But I needed a job, a house in which we could live, and an alternative career there being no guarantee that the Catholic Church would ever agree to my being ordained a Catholic priest. The future was very uncertain and I was afraid.

Alison, on the other hand, while recognising the problems had faith that it would all be resolved in God's good time.

Monsignor Aitken introduced me to three men who ultimately made it all possible from a financial point of view. These men were Peter Taylor, Bernie Pittman and Des Bowler, all members of the Knights of the Southern Cross and all associated with Southern Cross Homes. They were all told on a confidential basis what I was proposing to do and asked me what I thought I would want to do by way of employment. I proposed Southern Cross Bioethics Institute. To my astonishment Bernie Pittman had already been thinking about such a development at Southern Cross Homes having heard a paper I had given at a conference he had run on aged care.[21] Bernie Pittman and Peter Taylor were both convinced that there was a need for a Bioethics Institute that should not just deal with aged care issues but with all the bioethical issues confronting contemporary society. These three men saw to it that the Institute was established – and in that sense my family and I had a safe landing.

This is not to say that life was easy. On the contrary, I incurred significant debt in making the move, had a huge mortgage to pay (things were bad in Australia from 1987-1990 with very high interest rates), and I suffered from a loss of identity and the need to rebuild a new career. It also meant holding down a full-time job and doing my PhD on a full-time basis as well. Money was in very short supply for us, with Alison going out in the evenings selling Tupperware while I studied and looked after you girls. Of course your mother is a music teacher, but she had the care of you girls during the day

---

21 As Rector of The Church of the Good Shepherd, Anglican Parish Church of Plympton, I also had responsibilities to the Anglican residents at Southern Cross Homes. As a result of that involvement and my public reputation as a bioethicist, Bernie Pittman had asked me to contribute a paper to this conference.

making a resumption of her teaching career impossible at that stage. Conversion is not a road for the faint-hearted, particularly if you have been a minister of a Protestant ecclesial community, and it is just as well you cannot foresee all of the practical problems or you would never make the move.

But I can say this; I do not know what I would have done without Peter Taylor, Bernie Pittman and Des Bowler. Peter Taylor, in particular, as Chairman of the Board of Southern Cross Homes, went out of his way to ensure my family was safe and remained a steadfast friend until his death in May 2008.

So, God is good. In the 1990s financially better times finally arrived, you children were older and Alison could return to her profession as a music teacher, leaving behind the burdens of being a Tupperware salesperson. Somehow we survived it all.

This is how it happened

Two weeks before the announcement we told Grandma what we were going to do. My mother took it remarkably well. The next weekend she told us that she completely approved, had herself thought of becoming a Catholic when she was 19, but had ended up marrying an Anglican priest. Now widowed, she wanted to become a Catholic as well. I couldn't believe it! Apparently it is something she first considered when she was 19 (ie in 1930), but it had all seemed too difficult then and when she married an Anglican priest it faded from her mind. Now she had the opportunity and she took it. So the arrangements were made with Father Aitken and the time began to click down.

Archbishop Rayner was one of the few who knew what was in my mind and he faithfully kept the matter confidential as I requested. Confidentiality was extremely important to me as I knew that once the story 'leaked' it would soon become a major news story. Such is the price of being a 'media person'.

I had had a number of interviews with Archbishop Rayner in which I was treated very respectfully but was given no real reason, persuasive to me, as to why I should reconsider my position. In fact I was confirmed in my conviction that the Anglican Communion was a Protestant ecclesial community whose ordained ministers were almost certainly not validly ordained Catholic priests. He rehearsed the usual Protestant objections to the Papacy in entirely consequentialist terms, such as the issuing of the Syllabus of Errors.[22] A Pope said or did this which we enlightened ones know to be false so why make the move? The fact that Jesus Christ had endowed Peter with the keys to the kingdom of heaven and given him his teaching authority was never seriously discussed between us. Nevertheless, I was grateful to Archbishop Rayner for his kindness, his respectfulness, and his willingness to listen.

My parish knew nothing of it until the day of the announcement. How could I tell them until I was ready to go? As Easter arrived the depression deepened and I was virtually unable to function, getting my then Curate, Father John Hepworth, to celebrate all of the principal liturgies of the Triduum.

In Easter week I gave the story to Eddie Doogue of the Melbourne *Age*, and, of course, to the *Advertiser* for whom I was a columnist and had been for nearly 13 years. In this way I was able to get my version of the story straight with the reporters so that it could be accurately told. Eddie Doogue was brilliant and the *Advertiser* nearly as good. They faithfully reported that I had left the Anglican Church over the question of authority, not the ordination of women which had been the catalyst to a complete rethink of my position.[23] It was not that I did not love the Anglican Church, but that I loved the Church of Rome more, that I was "proud of my upbringing" and felt "a deep sense of gratitude to the Anglican Church for nurturing me in Catholic faith and practice". However, I said, that

> I now believe that it is only in Communion with the Bishop
> of Rome that I can be truly Catholic, and that the Catholic
> Church subsists in those Churches which are in full

22 "The name given to two series of propositions containing modern religious errors condemned respectively by Pius IX (1864) and Pius X (1907)". Cf the Catholic Encyclopedia at http://www.newadvent.org/cathen/14368b.htm.
23 Cf Public Statement by Father John I Fleming, undated but drafted on or about the 20 April 1987, and Statement to Parishioners of the Church of the Good Shepherd, Plympton, 26 April 1987.

communion with the Bishop of Rome. When such truths
are recognised only one course of action is possible.[24]

I made my announcement to the parish on the first Sunday after
Easter, resignation effective immediately. The Monday morning
editions of the papers concerned ran the story as did other papers
as well. I gave one or two radio interviews but no TV interviews
even though my house was surrounded by television cameras and
reporters from early in the morning until lunch time. To get away I
left via the back door and out through a gate in the back fence. I was
in no condition to talk to anyone.

That night your mother, Grandma, and I were all received into Full
Communion with the Catholic Church and a whole new life began.
I was no longer a clergyman. I was a Catholic layman.

The immediate aftermath – pleasant and unpleasant

One of the most gratifying things to happen was the deluge of mail
from well-wishers within the Catholic Church. Many of these came
from priests and women religious as well as laypeople.

One of these letters came from the Hon John Burdett, now
deceased, but then a Member of the Legislative Council. He wrote
on behalf of his wife as well as himself. They, too, were converts
from Anglicanism. In this letter he said:

> Jean and I were overjoyed at the news of your
> decision to seek reception into the One Holy
> Catholic Apostolic and Roman Church.
> ... We note the reference in the press to the
> ordination of women. We think we understand
> your position. It is not these particular issues
> which are the basis on which one leaves the
> Church of England. It is these issues which force
> us fundamentally and with complete intellectual
> honesty to examine our own faith and the position
> of the Anglican Church ... In our case, our

---

24 Public Statement by Father John I Fleming, undated but drafted on or about the
20 April 1987.

conversion was accompanied by deep emotional disturbance mainly because of family hostility. This was probably the most traumatic period of our life and it is certainly a time when a couple very greatly appreciate each other. At times it almost seemed that we had no one else, at a human level, except each other.[25]

This was a most perceptive set of comments from John Burdett particularly in light of the welter of claims made by people, some of whom worked for the media, who had such an ideological and emotional investment in the women's ordination issue that they were not prepared to give consideration to what I was saying were the real issues.

I also received a letter from Father (now Bishop) Geoffrey Jarrett, Administrator of St Mary's Cathedral, Hobart, who was then a complete stranger to me. He welcomed me and my family as we entered into full communion with the Catholic Church just as he had done twenty years previously. "I was received into the Catholic Church having reached those same conclusions in conscience that you have recently expressed. I know something of the pain and practical difficulties that are immediately consequent upon such a step ..."[26]

But there were at least two traumatic moments that reinforced for me that I had taken the way of the cross. I had been writing for the Adelaide *Advertiser*, the main daily paper in Adelaide, for many years as an op ed contributor. I had been aware of the hostility to my Christian views by certain other members of staff but had naively imagined that true liberals would always defend the rights of others to freedom of expression. In fact I came into possession of one internal communication within the paper from another contributor (who saw no problem in he himself being able to express his own views) objecting to my being able to explain what he considered my "conservative Christian views".

The consequence of this intervention was to see half of my

---

25 Personal correspondence, 27 April 1987.
26 Personal correspondence, 8 May 1987.

contributions being given to another 'liberal' writer who subsequently abandoned Christianity completely. The day after I was received into the Catholic Church I was summoned to a meeting with two of the editors responsible for the opinion pages. The purpose of the meeting was to inform me that now that I was a Catholic, things had changed. I had been appointed because I was an Anglican and wasn't the Anglican Church the biggest Church in South Australia? Well, no, the Catholic Church was. Well I had now changed hadn't I? Well no, I held the same views that day as I had for the weeks and months before. But what about contraception? I asked them whether they were enquiring about my sex life. Was I in favour of a legal ban on the sale of contraceptives? No. Would I write and say that? No. Why not? Because it was simply not a topical issue! Wouldn't Archbishop Faulkner now have to vet my pieces? Don't be ridiculous. In any case I would now be involved in internal censorship? So what responsible adult doesn't think before he speaks?

The bottom line was that I lost my position with the *Advertiser* at a time when the money was important to my family's livelihood, and on the basis of what I perceived to be a rank anti-Catholic prejudice.

The other traumatic moment came from within the Church itself. There were some at the highest level within the Church who, it appears, objected to the way Monsignor Aitken had brought me and my family into the Church. Someone drafted a document meant to describe the process by which any future Protestant minister would be received into the Church. Apart from the suggestion that such ordained ministers should be received via the RCIA programme,[27] effectively treating these ordained ministers as if they were no more Christian than an unbaptised person, the most offensive provision was this:

> There are times when such ordained ministers might be asked whether God is calling them to remain in their own church and to work vigorously for full communion

---

27 "RCIA stands for the Rite of Christian Initiation of Adults. It is a formal process whereby those who are unbaptised, are assisted in joining the Catholic Church by receiving what is called the Sacraments of Initiation." Catholic Archdiocese of Sydney website http://www.rcia.org.au/about.html.

between the churches.[28]

Not only is this contrary to the teachings of the Catholic Church, it represented to me a very hurtful rejection for me and my family. But I am grateful that, as far as I know, such draft policies were never official policies of the Archdiocese. In any case, Archbishop Faulkner never at any time suggested to me that he was anything other than pleased with the way things had been handled and had personally written to me welcoming me into the Catholic community. Nevertheless I had been made painfully aware from this and certain other statements coming from very senior people that not everyone was glad to have me in the Catholic Church because I was seen to be "very conservative", "right wing", and in any case opposed to women's ordination and the compulsory use of "inclusive language". Such is life.

But that negativity, hurtful and all as it was, was vastly outweighed by the kindness and goodness of the overwhelming majority of Catholic priests, the majority of religious women, and the almost unanimous support of the Catholic faithful who could not have been more welcoming.

Conclusion

I have been a Catholic for more than 23 years. In that time I have been ordained a Catholic priest (since 1995), made a Corresponding Member of the Pontifical Academy for Life (The Vatican) (since 1996), served as Foundation Director of Southern Cross Bioethics Institute in Adelaide (1987-2004), South Australia, and President of Campion College Australia from 2004 until 2008. How well God has looked after me and my family!

You see girls I know that I am where I really belong spiritually, and remain grateful to the Church for the forgiveness of all my sins through the powerful ministry of her ordained priests. This sense of certitude where the sacraments are concerned remains a deep source of comfort to me despite all my regrets for my past sins, for my weakness of will, and for my willingness to put off the 'evil day'

28 Personal correspondence, 14 September 1987.

in the hope that I could have both Catholicism and my attachment to Anglicanism which was personal, cultural, and spiritual.

But I really hope that you can see what I can see, the truth in all its glory in the Catholic religion.

As it is I now understand with even greater clarity than when we converted that the Catholic Church is the One True Church which Christ founded upon Peter and the other Apostles, and the only place spiritually speaking I can call home. Here I can really love God, love Our Lady and all the saints, and have the great privilege of knowing my sins are forgiven and that I am most truly receiving the Body and Blood of Christ in the offering of the Most Holy Sacrifice of the Mass.

2
Priestly celibacy and a married Catholic priest

Eight years after I was received into the Catholic Church I was ordained a Catholic priest. Rebecca has suggested to me that I need to say something about priestly celibacy and the fact that I am an exception to that rule, a married priest within the Latin rite. In this short essay I am responding to the various questions that have been put to me, my wife, and my daughters over the last 15 years on this subject.

Let me begin then at the beginning. I was brought up Anglican. Celibacy for the clergy is optional in Anglicanism. Most Anglican bishops, priests, and deacons are married. In the Anglican culture, a priest is someone who is married. My father was a priest. My Uncle Bill Fleming was a priest. Accordingly, the most natural thing in the world for me was the idea that a priest is someone who is married and has a family, accepting of course, that there were some priests who were unmarried.

At one point in my life I briefly considered whether God was calling me to the religious life and so to a life of celibacy. I quickly concluded that that was not my calling and always imagined that I would marry and have a family.

In the early 1970s I was happy as an Anglican priest, believed that the ecumenical movement between the Anglican Communion and the Catholic Church was well on track, and had no intention of being anything other than an Anglican despite my misgivings. So when Alison and I fell in love and decided to marry it was just a normal thing for us to do. We had no idea what the future held for us in terms of the Catholic Church. We were Anglican.

Of course, I was aware that some married Anglican priests in Western Australia had become Catholic priests following a dispensation allowing this to occur by Pope Paul VI. I was also aware that the same Pope in his 1967 encyclical on clerical celibacy in the Latin rite of the Catholic Church had also formalised the exceptions that might apply to ordained ministers of Protestant ecclesial communities who became Catholics:

> In virtue of the fundamental norm of the government of the Catholic Church, to which We alluded above, while on the one hand, the law requiring a freely chosen and perpetual celibacy of those who are admitted to Holy Orders remains unchanged, on the other hand, a study may be allowed of the particular circumstances of married sacred ministers of Churches or other Christian communities separated from the Catholic communion, and of the possibility of admitting to priestly functions those who desire to adhere to the fullness of this communion and to continue to exercise the sacred ministry. The circumstances must be such, however, as not to prejudice the existing discipline regarding celibacy.
>
> And that the authority of the Church does not hesitate to exercise her power in this matter can be seen from the recent Ecumenical Council, which foresaw the possibility of conferring the holy diaconate on men of mature age who are already married.
>
> All this, however, does not signify a relaxation of the existing law, and must not be interpreted as a prelude to its abolition.[29]

---

29 *Sacerdotalis caelibatus*, 24 June 1967, nn 42-43.

However, at that time I had not the slightest intention of leaving the Anglican Church and while all this was of course very interesting to me, it did not directly concern me at that time. In any case in 1967 I was only 24 years old and not yet ordained.

Alison and I married on the 4 January 1975. We were both happy as Anglicans at that stage, despite my intellectual issues, and I certainly believed that I would live out my days as a married Anglican priest. We would have children and be a family. Within two years of marriage we decided to go to England and I have described that part of my life in the previous chapter.

When Alison and I decided to become Catholics we knew that there was a possibility of my being ordained a Catholic priest because of the precedents set by Pope Pius XII, Pope Paul VI, and Pope John Paul II. In 1951 Pope Pius XII allowed the first such dispensation in modern times, in this case involving a married Lutheran Pastor. At the same time I knew and believed that no man had the right to be ordained, no matter what precedents existed. I knew that I had to be a Catholic and was prepared to be a layman in the Church if that was the Church's decision.

We also knew that in other parts of the Catholic Church there were married priests. This is the case in the Lebanese Catholic Churches (Maronite and Melchite rites), the Ukrainian and other Eastern Rite Catholic Churches. In these Churches bishops may ordain married men to the priesthood, but once a man is ordained a priest he may not then marry.

But why did I not simply content myself with being a Catholic layman? Why did I seek ordination as a Catholic priest in the Latin rite even though I knew that celibacy was the norm for priests in the that rite? Well, I had since the age of 19 believed I had a vocation to the priesthood. When I became a Catholic in 1987 nothing had changed. I still believed that God was calling me to be a priest. That being the case I had an obligation to present myself to the Church for consideration. If the Church said "no" I would have accepted that my vocation had not been verified by the Church. In which case, I would have seen myself free to pursue another career. Anyone who sincerely believes God is calling him to be a priest should present himself to the bishop. If the bishop, speaking in the name of the Church, does not accept him, then it would mean his vocation has not been verified by objective authority.

I sought ordination in the Latin rite because I am a Westerner and did not belong culturally to an Eastern Rite Catholic Church. Ordination would have to be in the Latin rite or not at all. And so I made my application which was considered by the Archdiocese of Adelaide within two years of my becoming a Catholic.

Archbishop Faulkner, Catholic Archbishop of Adelaide, was favourably disposed, very supportive, and the model of pastoral care and kindness to me and to my family. Nevertheless, the decision ultimately had to be made in Rome. That process took six years. Given that I was a Catholic two years before the process was initiated, I was a Catholic layman for eight years.

The process was protracted and a very difficult one. While I did not believe that I had a right to ordination I did have the right to an answer and, in my view, a reasonably speedy one. Eight years was a very long wait, one I was able to endure because of the strong support provided me by the priests of the Archdiocese of Adelaide. Especially helpful to me apart from Archbishop Faulkner were Monsignor Robert Aitken and Father (now Monsignor) Robert Egar. I cannot speak highly enough of the diocesan Catholic priests and many religious priests, sisters (especially the Dominicans), and brothers who prayed for us and offered all kinds of support to Alison and me.

Indeed it is fair to say that before my ordination and after, I received nothing but the warmest possible welcome from the Catholic clergy. Some have asked me whether there was any resentment directed at me from my brother priests and I can honestly say no. On the contrary, they accept me as a brother priest and are especially kind to my wife and children.

Where the laypeople of the Diocese are concerned, the same warm, and I would even say affectionate, welcome awaited me. I have already mentioned the support we received from the Knights of the Southern Cross, especially the late Peter Taylor, the late Des Bowler and Bernie Pitman. But wherever I have been as a Catholic priest, in the Archdiocese of Adelaide or the Diocese of Parramatta (where I now live), laypeople have been very accepting and very warm. This same warmth has greeted me wherever I have gone in the world and especially in the Vatican itself. As a Corresponding Member of the Pontifical Academy for Life I have been able to contribute to the work of the Academy as a priest and a scholar without any restriction or sense that I was anything other than just another Catholic priest.

Disagreement

Having said that, there are some who disagree with the ordination of a married man, but not always for the same reasons. One small group demonstrated at my ordination to the diaconate and my ordination to the priesthood. Two separate issues were at stake. One part of the group was opposed on the basis of their support for women's ordination. Why should the Pope grant such an exception when he would not consider the rights of women to be ordained? The other group were concerned that it seemed unjust to them that I, as a married man, could be ordained a priest, but what about those Catholic priests who had left to get married? Why couldn't they be brought back into service?

Of course the ordination of women and the ordination of a married man are really quite different issues. After all, St Peter was a married man and was called by Christ to be an apostle. But Christ did not call women to the priesthood. I suspect that the real agenda here was more political and personal, that since I had always opposed women's ordination when a priest in the Anglican Church and was thought to be theologically "conservative", it was a protest against my ordination in principle and an opportunity to promote women's ordination. The same group kept up these demonstrations for a few years but are now greatly diminished in numbers and energy.

Other people argued that the Church should first bring back "its own" priests who had left the active priesthood for marriage. Archbishop Faulkner patiently pointed out to these people on many occasions that while the Church has always been able to ordain married men to the priesthood, priests had never been allowed to marry. So a condition of my being ordained a Catholic priest, for instance, is that I had to agree that if my wife predeceased me, I could not marry again. Of course I accepted that condition willingly and without reservation.

One demonstrator at my ordination to the diaconate, a religious sister, carried a placard saying "Marriage for all priests". This led a priest friend of mine to remark: "So now marriage for priests is to be compulsory is it?"

These activists were, in fact, few in number, with some of the demonstrators not actually being themselves members of the Catholic Church. The vast majority of priests, religious and lay people found my ordination unproblematic and have warmly and gladly accepted me as a priest.

Marriage and Priestly Ministry

I am often asked what difference being married makes to being a Catholic priest. I find this very difficult to answer since I have never been a celibate priest. I am a very happily married man with a wonderful wife and three daughters each of which is the apple of their father's eye! My relationship with them bears no comparison to my relationship with anyone else. Alison is my best friend and life's partner. I enjoy a very close relationship with my daughters. And yet they have to share me with lots of other people with whom I may have a close pastoral relationship and who can make a call upon my time.

Speaking personally, I do not find it difficult to be like this but it may be more difficult for my family.

Each priest has his own gifts and abilities and it is idle, in my opinion, to compare myself with someone else. There are so many celibate priests and bishops that I greatly admire and who are so very good to me that I cannot imagine the Church without celibate priests. I know I am an exception where celibacy is concerned but I still do what other priests do. I am no better and no worse.

Does that mean I believe the Church should abandon celibacy as the norm for Catholic priests in the Latin rite? No. Now I know that some will say that I have the best of both worlds and am therefore somehow disqualified from having an opinion. But that assumes that the life of celibacy is not a "good" life. But clearly it is a good life, although not a life for everyone. The idea that marriage will somehow miraculously overcome sexual deviance in a man is insulting to women and clearly contradicted by reality.

Moreover celibate priests are able to move about more freely because a married priest must also take into account the needs of his wife and children. And, since a married priest and his family costs far more to support than a celibate priest, the question that has to be faced is this: which social programmes of the Church would need to be curtailed to pay for married priests who, as a matter of social justice, need to be paid a just wage. Apart from all of that there is an overriding importance to be attached to the idea that a celibate priest even more fully participates in the priesthood of Christ since Christ himself was celibate.

In the end it is others who must judge if being married has added anything or subtracted anything from their experience of me as a priest. While some may say that they feel freer to discuss sexual and marital issues with me because I am married the fact of the matter is that excellent support and advice is given to married people by celibate priests. In my experience celibate priests are just as capable of giving that advice as any married priest. But what I can certainly say is that while there are other pathways to maturity including the way of celibacy, I am, I believe, a better person as a result of my marriage to Alison and being the father of three daughters. They have all helped me enormously in growing and maturing as a man, and that, of course, can only be beneficial for my work as a priest which they have always totally supported.

3
Anglican Chaos –
Self-Inflicted Wounds

The current crisis in the Anglican Communion is still being fuelled by the ordination of women. The recent decision (July 2008) of the Church of England to ordain women bishops has further contributed to the difficulties facing the prospects of that Church's reunion with Rome. It also seems it will be the cause of another exodus of bishops, priests and laypeople from the Church of England into the Catholic Church. In the last chapter I referred to the debate on the ordination of women in the Anglican Church of Australia. Anglicanism as it was traditionally known and practised is in a state of disintegration. All that has changed over the last 21 years is that more Anglicans are being forced to confront, as I had to do, the fundamental questions of authority which are exposed by the women's ordination issue. Put another way, what is this debate really all about, and who is the 'umpire' who adjudicates it? I determined that the Pope and the Magisterium of the Catholic Church alone had the authority of Christ to resolve such fundamental matters of faith.

Because of the challenge deliberately thrown down to me in 1976 by Archbishop Keith Rayner, Anglican Archbishop of Adelaide and enthusiastic advocate of women's ordination, I was led to review for myself the literature on this issue in light of the fact that the Protestant Episcopal Church of the USA (Anglican) (July 1976) and the Anglican Church of Canada (October 1976) had decided to ordain women. The New Zealanders followed soon after. At about the same time the Sacred Congregation for the Doctrine of the Faith issued the document Inter Insigniores, Declaration on the Admission of Women to the Ministerial Priesthood (15 October 1976).

The arguments used in *Inter Insigniores* were, in my view, compelling. One by one the document examined the arguments used in favour of women's ordination, found them wanting, and replaced them with fundamental reasons why women could not be ordained and backed these up by better theological arguments. Thirty years later Sister Sara Butler MSBT, in her book T*he Catholic Priesthood and Women: A Guide to the Teaching of the Church* (Chicago. Hillenbrand Books, 2006), distinguished the fundamental reasons for the Church's teaching from the theological explanations offered for those fundamental reasons. She did this by reference to Inter Insigniores (1976) and Pope John Paul II's *Ordinatio Sacerdotalis* (1994).

But in 1976 at least I had *Inter Insigniores* together with the raft of Anglican literature consistent with it from orthodox Anglican theologians such as John Saward and Eric Mascall, and earlier writers such as C.S. Lewis. The arguments advanced by the Anglican bishops against the 'fundamental reasons' set out in *Inter Insigniores* were thin by comparison and rested upon Protestant assumptions about the sacred ministry, secular presuppositions about "equality", a Whig view of history,[30] and an extraordinary self-confidence in their own personal "infallibility". The Anglicans were proposing to do what the Church had never done, and never mind the people's rights to certitude where the sacraments are concerned. After all, you can't have it both ways. You cannot insist that the sacrament of Holy Communion is necessary for salvation[31] and at the same time experiment with the ordination of women to the priesthood, an office fundamentally necessary for the sacrament of the Lord's Supper to be validly consecrated. Or can you?

According to Anglican formularies the sacrament of Holy Orders

---

30 The term 'Whig' was originally coined to refer to "those accounts of our British past which celebrated it as revealing a continuous, on the whole uninterrupted, and generally glorious story of social and political progress, all leading up to the triumph of freedom and liberty.

31 *Vid.*, The Catechism, part of the Book of Common Prayer (1662), which contains the statement that there are only two sacraments generally necessary to salvation, Baptism and the Lord's Supper.

is one of those things "commonly called Sacraments" which are not be "counted for Sacraments of the Gospel ...[they] have not like nature of Sacraments with Baptism and the Lord's Supper".[32] So is the priesthood in Anglicanism a real sacrament or not? Well, as I soon discovered, it depends on who you talk to.

The conundrum for me, however, was that many Anglican bishops, including those that supported women's ordination to the priesthood, affected to believe a Catholic account of ordination, but behaved, in fact, in an entirely Protestant manner where Holy Orders were concerned. Why do I say "affected" to believe in the Catholic and Apostolic ministry? Well, apart from the fact that that is what I had always been taught, it was also the teaching of the 1973 "Canterbury Statement" produced as an agreed statement on Ministry and Ordination by the Anglican Roman Catholic International Commission, the very Commission set up by the Pope and the Archbishop of Canterbury to work toward full sacramental communion between the Catholic Church and the Anglican Communion.

As I say, following the encounter with Archbishop Rayner, I began to do my own research and reading on this controverted and controversial subject. Why? Because it was a challenge, involved a matter of truth fundamental to a Catholic understanding of the sacred priesthood of which I then believed myself to be a member, and because as a member of the Diocesan Synod (and later the General Synod of the Anglican Church of Australia) I would be called upon to cast a vote on the subject.

Personal attacks and silly arguments

As I became more closely involved in the debate on women's ordination I soon became subject to the personal (ad hominem) attacks of the proponents who always wanted to suggest that there must be something psychologically wrong with anyone who disagreed with them. But as far as I was concerned it had nothing to do with any alleged belief in the constitutional 'inferiority' of women, a rather

---

32 Article XXV of The Articles of Religion of the Church of England.

stupid and crass accusation often made against me by ideological feminists. Nor had it anything to do with something "my father did to me" as a former Anglican Rector of Glenelg so impudently suggested to me one night.

It is amazing how often I heard the psychologising argument used against opponents of women's ordination by otherwise intelligent people. The most egregious account of this line of 'reasoning' (and I use the word 'reasoning' advisedly!) was that the real reason men objected to women's ordination was 'menstruation'. Yes, menstruation! At a meeting of the "Parity Group" in London in 1978 I actually heard the women on the panel make that suggestion. In question time I asked about this extraordinary proposition and pondered aloud whether the desire by women for ordination could not be better explained in Freud's terms of "penis envy". Alison thought I might have gone a little far, but one of those women at least had the decency to approach me afterwards and take the point I was making: if you psychologise your 'opposition' don't be surprised if they do the same to you!

Anyway, for better or for worse I decided to take on the battle over women's ordination, head on. I was interested to see what the arguments really were rather than the silly and seriously ill-mannered stuff I was hearing from Christian feminists. My friend Father Geldard has a videotape of a woman being interviewed about why she was not allowed to be a priest. She said: "I suppose it's because I don't have a penis!" There we go again! But there were people making some serious arguments and they had to be dealt with. The one I took most seriously was my own Archbishop, Keith Rayner, a man of prodigious intellectual ability who would always listen carefully to those with whom he disagreed.

Rayner the 'Whig historian'

The term 'Whig' was originally coined to refer to "those accounts of our British past which celebrated it as revealing a continuous, on the whole uninterrupted, and generally glorious story of social and political progress, all leading up to the triumph of freedom and liberty."[33] Put another way, 'Whig" historians believe in the march of progress such that we move onwards and upwards to better and better social and political conditions. In the context of the Anglican Church of Australia the number one intellectual supporting the ordination of women was undoubtedly Keith Rayner and he was described as a 'Whig historian', by fellow historian David Wetherell.

Rayner certainly believed that the ordination of women would simply "make explicit what is latent in Christianity", but he also used history in a way that suggested this development was inevitable. Wetherell refers to two addresses given by Rayner, then Archbishop of Adelaide, in 1985. Here

> ... the sweep of church history is surveyed in such a way as to imply that the women's ordination question is but the latest example of the pattern of responses which the church has always presented to the imperatives of history. First, the church responds with stubborn resistance: but then it acts with compliance as it realises that further resistance is useless.[34]

That Archbishop Rayner held this view of history was graphically revealed to me when we travelled back to Adelaide together from Sydney after the General Synod of 1985. He spoke to me about "the great watersheds" of history, which included the agreement of the Council of Jerusalem (Acts 15) not to impose circumcision on Gentile men who wished to be Christians, and a range of other such great events culminating in the ordination of women. Perhaps Wetherell is inclined to a kinder view of this approach to history than me. I saw in it a crude Marxism with the Church helpless before the inexorable forces of history which make 'revolution' inevitable. In this approach Rayner was joined by Archbishop Penman, then Archbishop of Melbourne, who called women's ordination "inevitable".[35]

All of this was very much in keeping with the 'spirit of the age'

---

33 David Wetherell, "The uses of History in the Women's Ordination Debate", in David Wetherell ed., *op. cit.*, 75-76.
34 *Ibid.*, 74-75.
35 *Church Scene* 7 February 1986 and cited in David Wetherell, *ibid.*, 75.

in which we lived, with the ordination of women as less a theological matter than a political one which could be decided by appeal to 'justice for women' and 'equal opportunity'.

But Dr Rayner has a very sharp mind. He could see that the historical analysis of which he was so fond wouldn't cut it by itself. He needed to show that women's ordination was not only theologically possible but, really, necessary, that past theological understandings were defective and, most importantly, that the Anglicans had the authority to decide the matter of women's ordination and proceed to such ordinations in the event of an affirmative decision by its Synods. Dr Rayner took his opposition seriously and engaged the contra arguments better than any other advocates of women's ordination in Australia.

Rayner the theologian

Dr Rayner was a well-trained academic with an earned PhD. Nevertheless I found significant errors in his theological reasoning, errors which really disconcerted me. One of these errors was his allegation that the Catholic Church believed that women were defective men. I heard this from him on a number of occasions, and he used it to good effect in the debate at the General Synod held in August 1987, some three months after I had become a Catholic.

In her report on the debate in her book, *Women in the Church,* the contemporary Melbourne historian Muriel Porter says that the Anglo-Catholic opponents of women's ordination were restrained "with no John Fleming to give the Anglo-Catholic opposition real bite"[36], while the Evangelicals were frightening horses in the street with their argument based on the headship of husband vis-à-vis his wife and how the natural order of things would be disrupted by women's ordination. Porter is undoubtedly accurately representing the mood of the 1987 Synod. But, it reflected very badly on the liberals who belong to a Church that proudly claims it is "Biblical" when they so illiberally refused to give proper weight to the Biblical arguments that sincere Evangelicals were presenting, especially when

---

36 Muriel Porter, *op. cit.,* 130.

those arguments were being presented in a very scholarly way by
Bishop Paul Barnett of Sydney. Similar arguments based upon the
same passages of Scripture, and expressed differently, have been and
still are held to be persuasive by many Catholic scholars.[37]

But it was Archbishop Rayner who was responsible for one of the
more egregious theological mistakes. For example, in her description
of the speakers on the other side who take up the headship question,
Muriel Porter portrayed Rayner as a "formidable debater". Rayner,
she said, "referred to St Thomas Aquinas' belief that women were
defective men, lacking the fullness of humanity. This belief," he
maintained, "was no longer acceptable."[38]

Well it was never acceptable, least of all to St Thomas Aquinas.
No doubt Rayner picked up this mistake from feminist literature, but
he would have done better to have checked what Aquinas actually
said.

The reference to women as defective and misbegotten men
belongs, in fact, to Aristotle whose biological science was the only real
show in town at the time of Aquinas. Aquinas gives due deference
to Aristotle, as would anyone today give due deference to Albert
Einstein, but comes to very different conclusions.

> On the other hand, as regards human nature in general,
> woman is not misbegotten, but is included in nature's
> intention as directed to the work of generation. Now
> the general intention of nature depends on God, Who is
> the universal Author of nature. Therefore in producing
> nature, God formed not only the male but also the
> female.[39]

Moreover, in addressing the question of the relationship between
man and woman St Thomas also says:

---

37 Cf, for example, Patrick J Dunn, *Priesthood: A Re-examination of the Roman Catholic
Theology of the Presbyterate*, New York: Alba House 1990, 175-185; Manfred Haucke, *Women
in the Priesthood? A Systematic Analysis in the Light of the Order of Creation and Redemption*.
San Francisco: Ignatius Press, 1988.
38 *Ibid.*, 130.
39 *Summa Theologiae* I, q 92, article 1.

It was right for the woman to be made from the rib of man. First, to signify the social union of man and woman, for the woman should neither use authority over man, and so she was not made from his head; nor was it right for her to be subject to man's contempt as his slave, and so she was not made from his feet.[40]

St Thomas also observed that, "in the worldly sphere (*in temporalibus*), a woman can quite well function as ruler, but not in priestly spiritual matters (*in sacerdotalibus*)."[41]

How strange it is, then, for a leading advocate of women's ordination, to so completely misrepresent not only St Thomas but also what he imagines the teaching of the Church to have been all these centuries. The Angelic Doctor (a nickname for St Thomas Aquinas) was faithful to the way the Church in its tradition sees the relationship between the sexes.

In fact the pre-Christian Aristotle himself, although confused about the relationship between man and woman, was absolutely clear that women were not the slaves of men (unless they belonged to the class of slaves which included both men and women).[42] His thing about women being defective men was based upon his understanding of human reproductive biology, a biology which knew nothing of the ovum (egg) from the woman but only the seed (semen) from the man which was planted in the woman. Whatever of Aristotle's faulty biology, he only said women were defective men as it were. In Latin, Aristotle's view is expressed thus: *femina est mas occasionatus*. While the word *occasionatus* is not a word found in classical Latin, the theologians used it to mean something caused unintentionally or accidentally. So it certainly implied something defective in the woman. Nevertheless, this is rejected by Aquinas.

Although I have no recollection of Rayner saying it, some have attributed to Aquinas (and Aristotle) the view that the man receives

---

40 *Summa Theologiae* I, q 92, article 3.
41 *Summa Theologiae Supplement,* q 39 al ad 2/3 and cited in Manfred Haucke, *op. cit.,* 404.
42 Cf Aristotle, *Politica*, Book 1.2, 1252[b].

his soul at 40 days after conception and the woman 90 days after conception. This, too, is wrong. It is based on Aristotle's observation that a male embryo can be recognised as male at 40 days (if there has been a spontaneous abortion) and a female embryo after 90 days.[43] Aquinas refers to this passage, which says nothing about the infusion of a soul (*In 3 Sent.*, 3, 5, 2, co et ad 3). "He cites the passage because he wishes to argue that the body of Christ was complete in every detail, even if tiny, from the moment of conception, whereas other embryos are only gradually articulated. Neither in Aristotle's original statement nor in Aquinas' comment on it is there any reference to the infusion of the soul. There are more than fifty passages elsewhere in Aquinas where he does refer to the infusion of the rational soul. In none of these passages does he make any distinction between men and women."[44]

On many occasions Rayner referred to one of the sayings of that great Father of the Church, St Gregory Nazianzus. St Gregory was dealing with the heresy known as Docetism, the idea that Jesus was not really a man but only seemed to be a man. In line with St Paul's teaching about redemption coming through a man, St Gregory said: "That which he did not assume he did not redeem." In other words, if Jesus is not truly Man then mankind was not redeemed. Lifted out of its context, Rayner seemed to call St Gregory to his witness that women can and should be ordained since they too are redeemed. This would no doubt have come as a complete surprise to St Gregory. The Church does not ordain women despite her insistence on the radical equality of men and women under the New Dispensation. If Baptism is the only qualifier for candidacy for ordination, we have a ready made argument for the ordination of children!

Put another way, it was becoming clearer and clearer to me that the theological arguments being touted for women's ordination were nothing other than a smokescreen for the real agenda, which was in fact a contemporary Western political agenda linked to certain

---

43 Cf Aristotle, *History of Animals*, 3: 15-30.
44 Michael Nolan, "What Aquinas Never Said About Women" http://www.firstthings. com/article.php3?id_article=3594.

assumptions about the functionality of the office of priest and the feminist insistence that the issue was really all about, only about, equal opportunity. Rayner himself gives the game away when he says he does not support women's ordination because men and women are the same (a palpably silly proposition anyway since if they were the same the debate wouldn't have been happening), but because they are not the same. "And it is precisely because they are different they must be ordained. They will bring a complementarity needed in the ministry of the church."[45]

My concentrating on Archbishop Rayner's arguments is a sign of the respect that I had for him because, it seemed to me, he was women's ordination's most powerful and persuasive advocate in the Anglican Church of Australia at that time. Mutual respect continued between us and he wrote me a very warm letter of congratulations which I received the day before my ordination to the Catholic priesthood, a letter which I was pleased to receive and have kept.

Arguments against the 'fundamental reasons'

The Anglican debate, so it always seemed to me, was a mishmash of arguments, many frankly secular, and many directed to undermine the principal Biblical sources. For example, the Biblical fact is that Christ chose men only for the Twelve Apostles. This fact is wished away by saying, "Oh well, Christ was just a victim of his own sociological conditioning. In his day and age, he couldn't have done anything else!" Never mind that this assumes that proponents of women's ordination were not themselves "victims of their own sociological conditioning". And it certainly begs the question: "Who is more likely to be a victim of sociological conditioning, us or Jesus who according to Christian belief is God as well as Man?" Even worse, if it really is the case that Jesus is either a victim of sociological conditioning or, put more mildly, ready to compromise with the spirit of his age for fear of upsetting the locals, what other of Jesus' teachings and examples need to be reassessed, revised, or overturned because they accord only with the spirit of His age, not ours which is, of course, by definition 'wiser'! The Whig view of history rises again. And if

45 Muriel Porter, *op. cit.,* 130-131.

Jesus is the Word made flesh, the God-Man, how could He get it all so terribly wrong?[46]

Yet the fact of what Christ actually did remains as one of the principal reasons why women were not ordained, and that the only Christians in past centuries who promoted women's ordination were those belonging to heretical sects such as the Montanists in the second century, and the Collyridians in the fourth century.

It is not the place here to address all of the arguments against the "fundamental reasons" why women could not be admitted into the ministerial priesthood. The interested reader can consult a myriad of sources for that, with two in particular meriting special attention.[47] But there were, at least to me, some other factors which led me to see clearly that the ordination of women was not the ultimate goal of the Anglican and Protestant Reformers of the twentieth century.

Women's Ordination and the Challenge to the Doctrine of God

In the early 1980s I was introduced to William Oddie, Librarian at Pusey House, Oxford, UK. He was writing his important book in which he argued that the real agenda behind women's ordination was a radical reconstruction of the doctrine of God. When the book was published in 1984, the front cover bore an image of Christa, a naked female on a cross which had been set up in the Cathedral Church of St John the Divine (PECUSA) in New York. Within the covers of this explosive book Oddie, citing many quotations from the feminist Christian literature, exposes what the real agenda is. A couple of quotes serve to make the point.

> Conservatives are correct in recognising that the revolution represented by the ordination of women threatens the whole symbolic structure.[48]

---

46 For a much fuller explanation of all my concerns see John Fleming, "To The Intent That These Orders May Be Continued … ", in David Wetherell, *op. cit.*, 82-90.

47 Sara Butler MSBT, *The Catholic Priesthood and Women: A Guide to the Teaching of the Church*. Chicago: Hillenbrand Books, 2006; Manfred Haucke, 1988, *op. cit.*

48 Rosemary Radford Reuther, *New Woman, New Earth*, New York 1975, 79 and cited in William Oddie, *What Will Happen to God?: Feminism and the Reconstruction of Christian Belief*, London: SPCK, 1984, 11.

> If women rise up and assume the place they should
> legitimately have in society, that society will change and
> take on a different aspect … [But] what will happen to
> God if women in many churches demand the places that
> they should have in the structures of those churches, after
> having acquired clarity through their feminist criticism of
> religion … [there will be a] changing of the Gods.[49]

Add to this the disarmingly frank manner in which Harvey Cox,
author of *The Secular City*, put his point of view writing in favour of
women's ordination:

> Frightened conservatives, as usual, are partly right in the
> arguments they advance against the ordination of women.
> Unlike enlightened symbol-blind liberals, they know full
> well that this is not just an equal opportunity issue. Female
> priests would, despite themselves, modify the meaning
> of the Mass. But what conservatives fear, I welcome: a
> Christian sacrament enriched by the presence at the altar
> of the Great Mother, the Scarlet Woman, the Whore of
> Babylon and the Virgin Queen. So the conservatives are
> right in their panic but wrong in their conclusion.[50]

Official Catholic Teaching

Suffice it to say that *Inter Insigniores* laid out the Church's "fundamental
reasons" in four articles.

> The reasons are 1) that there is an unbroken, universal
> tradition of admitting only men to ministerial priesthood;
> 2) that this tradition is rooted in Christ's manner of
> acting, that is, his choice of men as his apostles; 3) that

49 Catharina Halkes, "The Themes of Protest in Feminist Theology against God the
Father", in JB Metz and E Schillebeeckx (eds), "God as Father", *Concilium* 143, New
York 1981, in William Oddie, *ibid.*, 16.
50 *New York Times* 1 October 1973, cited by MD Haverland in 'The Increasingly Serious
Obstacle: A Reply to Archbishop Carnley's "Eleven Theses on Maintaining, Extending,
and Deepening Our Communication In The Context of The Debate About The
Ordination of Women'", *The Anglican Society*, Perth, 1986:2.

this tradition was maintained by the apostles in fidelity
to his example; and 4) that this tradition is normative for
the Church.[51]

From the time of *Inter Insigniores* a debate continued within the
Catholic Church which was not finally brought to an end until the 22nd
of May 1994 (Pentecost Sunday), with the issuing of the Apostolic
Letter given by Pope John Paul II, *Ordinatio Sacerdotalis*. The Pope
concluded the discussion on women's ordination to the priesthood
in this way:

> Although the teaching that priestly ordination is to be
> reserved to men alone has been preserved by the constant
> and universal Tradition of the Church and firmly taught
> by the Magisterium in its more recent documents, at the
> present time in some places it is nonetheless considered
> still open to debate, or the Church's judgment that women
> are not to be admitted to ordination is considered to have
> a merely disciplinary force.
>
> *Wherefore, in order that all doubt may be removed regarding a
> matter of great importance, a matter which pertains to the Church's
> divine constitution itself, in virtue of my ministry of confirming the
> brethren (cf. Lk 22:32) I declare that the Church has no authority
> whatsoever to confer priestly ordination on women and that this
> judgment is to be definitively held by all the Church's faithful.*[52]
> (emphasis added)

Immediately following the publication of this Apostolic Letter,
theologians with a "tax lawyer's" mentality began questioning the
status of the Letter and whether the Pope was really saying that this
teaching on women's ordination was definitive. On the 28th October
1995 the Congregation for the Doctrine of the Faith issued a reply
(*Responsum*) to the doubt expressed (*Dubium*) by some theologians
as to whether or not the teaching presented "in the Apostolic Letter
Ordinatio Sacerdotalis to be held definitively, is to be understood as
belonging to the deposit of faith". The *Responsum* or reply was "In
the affirmative". The CDF went on to say this:

---

51 Sara Butler, *op. cit.*, 9.
52 *Ordinatio sacerdotalis*, n. 4.

This teaching requires definitive assent, since, founded on the written Word of God, and from the beginning constantly preserved and applied in the Tradition of the Church, it has been set forth infallibly by the ordinary and universal Magisterium (cf. Second Vatican Council, Dogmatic Constitution on the Church *Lumen Gentium* 25, 2). Thus, in the present circumstances, the Roman Pontiff, exercising his proper office of confirming the brethren (cf. Lk 22:32), has handed on this same teaching by a formal declaration, explicitly stating what is to be held always, everywhere, and by all, as belonging to the deposit of the faith.

The Sovereign Pontiff John Paul II, at the Audience granted to the Cardinal Prefect of the CDF, Joseph Cardinal Ratzinger, approved the Reply and ordered it to be published.

With the issuing of the *Responsum* to the *Dubium* in 1995, the debate on women's ordination was over. But that was eight years after Alison and I came into full communion with the Catholic Church, and about three years before women began to be ordained in the Anglican Church of Australia. So, if women's ordination was the issue, why did we jump the gun? The answer to that question is that neither of us left for that reason. To be sure it was a catalyst to our complete rethinking of the nature of the Church and where authority was mediated in the Church. The decisive reasons why we both decided to become Catholics was precisely because we came to believe the claims of the Catholic Church to be the true and authentic Church of Jesus Christ and the Apostles, and because we had come to recognise that Christ gave the Church a constitution which contained institutions through which His authority was to be mediated within the Church. Those institutions are the Petrine Office located in the Bishop of Rome and the College of Bishops acting in harmony with and with the consent of the Bishop of Rome.

And we both feel that our Catholic instincts which told us that women could not be ordained have been vindicated by the authoritative pronouncement of the Pope, a pronouncement which "is to be held always, everywhere, and by all, as belonging to the deposit of the faith."

4
Prologue to Part II

I have detailed an account of my conversion from Anglicanism to Catholicism and the way in which I have dealt with the question of women's ordination. I passionately believe in objective truth and especially objective truth about the nature of God and His plan for human beings, created in His own image and likeness.

I have always wanted to share what I have with others, and especially those for whom the Gospel of Jesus Christ, in its fullest understanding, seems difficult. I have dealt with the claims of the Catholic Faith at my own personal level. I will do so again in chapter 8 in the context the desire of a large group of Anglicans who were seeking a new way to be Anglican in the light of the disintegration of Anglicanism as it had always been known.

The fact is that I was, in the end, converted to Christianity by my experience of the Real Presence of Christ in the Eucharistic Sacrifice. Intellectual persuasion was, by itself, not enough. I needed a real experience of the living Lord Jesus Christ which I found in the Mass. This has been true for many other people I know and is therefore one of the principal reasons why I originally agreed to write these two essays.

Now, as a Catholic priest I have had the privilege of coming to know many fine young people for whom I have the greatest personal admiration. Two of these people are Robert and Mads. Robert is unbaptised, a young man of great personal integrity, but one for whom Christianity played little or no part in his life until he met Mads, a practising Catholic. Robert was open to Catholicism, but yet to be convinced. He was puzzled by two key elements of Catholic belief which affect the Mass, the central activity of Catholics. "You mean," he says, pointing to the Eucharistic Bread in the Monstrance on the altar, "that that is the Body of Jesus Christ?"

My ministry as a priest is not just about my own personal conversion, or the situation of my former co-religionists in the Traditional Anglican Communion, but all those with whom I come into contact.

These next two chapters on the Mass were written for them personally. They have been written to show how the miraculous dimension to Catholic Faith and practice accords with reason such that young people may be assisted to see that Catholicism is an intellectually and spiritually compelling religion which is objectively true and which satisfies the human desire to find a synthesis between faith and reason. When you experience the Real Presence of Christ effected by the change of bread and wine into the Body and Blood of Christ in the context of the Sacrifice of the Mass, you will also find a personal relationship with Christ which transforms your life.

In the hope of helping many other young people to come to know Christ personally in and through the Mass, as I and so many other Catholics have done, these next two chapters are now offered for a wider readership. They are included here because of my profound conviction that just as the Mass was the key to my own conversion to Christianity, and later, together with the issue of authority, to the fullness of the Catholic Faith, so it has been for all those Anglicans who belong to the TAC, and will be for many young people seriously considering the claims of the Gospel of Jesus Christ.

5

In What Sense is the Mass a Sacrifice?

I know what it is like to struggle with religion, belief in God, the Church, and the fundamental beliefs of Catholics. Transubstantiation is one of those teachings that most people find challenging, that quintessentially Catholic teaching that what appears as bread and wine is actually, really and truly, the Body and Blood of Jesus Christ.

But before I try to explain the doctrine of Transubstantiation I need first to explain the nature of the Mass, how it is that the Sacrifice of Calvary and the Sacrifice of the Mass are one and the same sacrifice, the first offered through the shedding of blood and the second offered sacramentally. So, Robert and Mads, if you will allow me, I will deal with the Sacrifice of the Mass now and in the next chapter with Transubstantiation.

To begin then, it is important to notice the strongly sacrificial language which Christ used at the Last Supper when the Eucharist was inaugurated. Taking bread he said, "This is my body which will be given up for you". Taking a cup of wine he said, "This is my Blood which will be shed for you", and "Do this in memory of me". These words not only make plain that the gifts of bread and wine are changed into Christ's Body and Blood, but that through the Eucharist we participate here and now in Christ's death and resurrection. St Paul was later to put it this way: "For as often as you eat this bread and drink the cup, you proclaim the Lord's death until he comes."[53]

To try and make sense of this Catholic teaching I will begin by describing what the word 'sacrifice' means and how it was used in the context of the Old Testament which forms the background against which we need to interpret what Christ intended.

The meaning of the word "sacrifice"

Much of the confusion about the meaning of the "Sacrifice of the Mass" comes about through a faulty and secular understanding of sacrifice which is now very much part of Western secular culture. Thus for most Australians 'sacrifice' has become synonymous with the giving up of one's life at a time of war or to help another person in trouble. It could also simply mean 'killing', as in sacrificing some animals in a scientific experiment. And there is an element of truth in those understandings. BUT the word is originally deeply religious and comes from two Latin words. The original single word is *sacrificium* and the two component words are these:

> a) *Sacrificus* ("performing priestly functions or sacrifices").
> *Sacrificus* comes from *sacra* ("sacred rites") which in turn comes from sacer ("sacred").
> b) *Facere* ("to do or perform")

So, in religious terms, the word "sacrifice" means performing a sacred act or rite. The word "rite" comes from the Latin word *ritus* ("religious observance or ceremony, custom, usage").

The word "sacrifice" stretches well beyond notions of "something, even life, given up for the sake of another." It is about performing sacred rites in order to worship God and to propitiate sin and guilt. It is very similar to the English word "offering". But the thing "offered" does not become a sacrifice until there is a real change in the visible gift itself, a point to which I will return later.

But now let us see what "sacrifice" meant in the first century AD, the time when Jesus was carrying out his earthly ministry.

---

53 1 Corinthians 11:26.

Abraham and Isaac

From the time of Abraham, the father of the Jewish nation, the Jewish people were different from the other nations. The religions of the other nations used human sacrifice as a way of appeasing the wrath of God. Abraham and Sarah were old and she was sterile. Leaving aside the child Ishmael who was fathered by Abraham through the slave woman Hagar, Abraham was ultimately to have a son through his wife Sarah. His name was Isaac. Through Isaac God's promise to Abraham was to be fulfilled, that Abraham was to be the Father of many nations. Problem: according to Abraham's religious upbringing he was meant to offer his first born son. In this case his son as a sacrifice. This is a great test of faith for Abraham and in obedience to God he begins to do what he believes is expected of him. He makes all the preparations necessary to kill his son and offer him as a sacrifice to God. But God intervenes to prevent this happening.

So it is that, following the example of Abraham, the Jews were a people that turned their collective backs on human sacrifice. And in preventing the death of Isaac, Abraham's only son, God ensured that his promise to Abraham could be fulfilled. But it is important to note that the notion of sacrifice itself was not abrogated. On the contrary, its importance was recognised and refocused. In place of Isaac God Himself provided the sacrifice, which was a "ram in a thicket". (You can read the story in Genesis 22:1-24) Many centuries later, God again provided the sacrifice. He provided His only Son as the Lamb who takes away the sins of the world and restores man's relationship with his Lord and God. In doing this God showed His love for human beings, providing a way in which they could both be reconciled to God and have the means by which they could worship God in the most perfect possible way. But I am getting ahead of myself.

Old Testament Sacrifices

Ever since the time when human beings rebelled against God they felt guilt and shame because of the sins they felt powerless to resist. They needed to find a way to say sorry to God, have their sins forgiven, and therefore be able to approach Him and worship Him. Sin and guilt offerings are a subset of sacrifice, the only means by which people could satisfy their deepest religious needs. They were looking for a way in which they could truly worship God. But what 'gift' could they offer God which would be in any way appropriate to Him who needs no gifts. The 'gift', the only gift they could offer, was life itself since this was the greatest gift that God had given human beings. But they could not slay a human being for that purpose. So they associated themselves with the life of the animal which was to be used in sacrifice. They laid their hands on the animal to demonstrate their personal identification with the sacrificial offering (cf Psalm 51:17). The death of the animal, the 'victim', also represented the death of the sinner to sin. The 'blood' of the animal was seen as the 'life' of the animal. Even today we still talk about the 'life blood'.

The slaying of the animal was really about the release of the 'life blood' which was gathered into a bowl and poured over an altar. The worshippers could not take this blood and use it for any other purpose. It belonged to God as the 'gift' offered with which was associated the one who had brought the animal to the priest. They believed that in this offering the barrier of sin between the sinner and God was broken down, and the sinner was restored to God's good grace. The animal was then roasted and eaten as a communion meal. It was a meal representing the fact that the sinner was now at one with God and with his neighbours who shared in the meal. This is where the word atonement comes from, i.e. being freed from the guilt of sin and therefore being made "at one" with God.

So, the life of the animal has been released (shedding of blood) and poured out over the altar as a sacrificial gift to God. The sacrifice cleanses sinners from sin, allows them to worship with the gift of their own lives which interiorly they have associated with the life of the animal. And the food received, the roasted flesh of the animal, was a sign of the power that God gives people, strengthening them to live out the life they have promised to live through the sacrifice. Yes, the animal is food for the body, but it is more importantly food for the soul. The animal is a sacrifice because there has been a real change in the gift, the blood being removed from the animal and given to God with the modified beast being returned to the one who offers the sacrifice as food for the body and the soul.

The Exodus and the 'Sacrifice of the Passover'

Intimately connected with the whole idea of the Sacrifice of the Mass is the Feast of the Passover, which is a memorial of the Exodus. The word "exodus" literally means "the way out". For the Jewish people it is the great event which established the fact that, as the chosen people of God, they were loved by God. That love was expressed in the deliverance of the Jewish people from a life of slavery in Egypt and the gift of the 'promised land'. Moses was appointed by God to lead His people. He confronted the Pharaoh (the king of Egypt) and demanded that he let the people go. Although punished by many plagues Pharaoh refused to free his slaves.

The climax of the confrontation between the God of Israel as represented by Moses and Pharaoh is called the Passover. The Hebrews are instructed by Moses to prepare themselves for this climactic event. They are to take a lamb and kill it. The blood is to be daubed on the two doorposts and the lintel of their houses. The blood of the lamb will protect them as the Angel of Death comes to kill the first born throughout the land. The Angel will 'pass over' their houses and they will be protected. They are to roast the lamb and eat it and they are to be dressed ready for travel, sandals on their feet and a staff in their hands. And when they have been freed and come to the "promised land" they are to "observe this rite as an ordinance"[54] Moreover, when their children ask them, "what do you mean by this service?", they are to reply, "It is the sacrifice of the Lord's Passover, for he passed over the houses of the people of Israel in Egypt, when he slew the Egyptians but spared our houses."[55]

The people did as they were commanded, the Angel came, and the first born of all the Egyptians were killed including the son of Pharaoh. The Pharaoh let the people go. The people leave Egypt, Pharaoh changes his mind and pursues them, and they are trapped by the Red Sea. God divides the sea, the people go across to the other side, and the Egyptians pursue them. God lets the sea return

---

54 Exodus 12:24.
55 Exodus 12:26-27.

and the Egyptians are drowned. And so the second meaning of the Passover is that the Jewish people pass over the Red Sea from slavery in Egypt into the freedom of the 'promised land'.

It was during the Feast of the Passover that Jesus instituted the Eucharist and again provides the context within which the Eucharist is to be understood. The Passover Feast was, and remains, central to the life of the Jewish people. They follow the ritual instructions set out in the Scriptures, eating unleavened bread and the sacrificial lamb. Thus the Passover Feast, which is a sacrifice, is the context of the Eucharist which, too, is a memorial of the new Passover where Christ is the sacrificial lamb, and the unleavened bread is the flesh which we eat.

Memorial in the Old Testament

When sacrifice was offered at the Feast of the Passover, the *seder* as it was known, the Israelites concerned re-enacted by word and action the covenantal sacrifice (the slaying of the lamb and the blood put on their houses to protect them from the Angel of Death), the Exodus from Egypt, and the wandering years in the desert. In this way the added dimension to the sacrifice is the participation in, or being caught up in, the great saving works of God in a *virtual* (and, in that way, a real) sense. The Exodus is made virtually present through the ritual acts of the *seder* or Passover Meal. "In the sense of Sacred Scripture the *memorial* is not merely the recollection of past events but the proclamation of the mighty works wrought by God for men."[56] So every time the Passover is celebrated, the memory of the Jewish believers is refreshed by the knowledge and fact of God's great saving events. Once again, they renew their pledge to conform their lives to the God who saved them. The *memorial* is then a making present of a past event so that one can really participate in that event here and now. So when Jesus said, "Do this in memory of me", he was telling his disciples that they were to do it and that in doing it they would be able to participate in his death and resurrection.

---

56 *Catechism of the Catholic Church* (CCC), 1363.

The Sacrifice of Jesus

The sacrifice of Jesus Christ only makes sense in terms of the Old Testament practice of sacrifice. His sacrifice is the fulfilment of the Old Testament sacrificial system.

1. In the Old Testament the priest and victim were separate from each other.
2. In the Old Testament the association of the believer with the sacrifice was only proximate and not real. That is, he associated himself with the animal by touching it, but he was not the animal.
3. Every time a person sinned in the Old Testament, another sacrifice had to be offered. This was because the blood of bulls and goats was not only ineffective in the short term but also in the longer term. Therefore, it had to be repeated even if one imagined it was effective in the short term.

But with the sacrifice of Jesus certain elements are crucially different:

1. Because Jesus is the representative human being, the Second Adam, He is God made Man (in the fullest generic sense). So as the sacrificial Victim He really incorporates us.
2. The sacrifice of Jesus is voluntary (cf animals).
3. The one who offers the sacrifice and the sacrifice offered are one and the same person (i.e. Jesus is both the Priest and the victim).[57]
4. Jesus' sacrifice is eternally efficacious. It happened in space and time but has now been removed from the confines of space and time through his resurrection and ascension into the heavenly sanctuary. As a result, all human beings in all times, places, and ages can have access to the reality and the effects of that sacrifice.

---

57 St Thomas Aquinas, *Summa Theologica*, III, q. 83, a. 1.

Jesus is the Lamb of Sacrifice and the Priest who offers that Sacrifice. He ascends into heaven, into the heavenly sanctuary where as Priest He offers Himself as the Lamb of Sacrifice to God the Father. All that He has done on earth, all that He has achieved, is now re-presented in heaven. This means that what Jesus began on a cross at Calvary is continued in eternity and is therefore able to be accessed by all human beings no matter in what historical period they live. So while the sacrifice of Calvary happened in space and time, it is not confined by space and time. Through the Eucharist Christ enables us to re-present, to offer the same sacrifice which He inaugurated on Calvary.

So Transubstantiation, the change of the whole substance of the bread and wine into the risen and ascended Body and Blood of Christ, the glorified Christ, is the guarantee of our being able to offer Him on the earthly altar in union with the Heavenly Altar. This is so because Jesus, the Lamb of Sacrifice who is in heaven, has now become present on our earthly altars.

Moreover, in the Old Testament the Jews ate the animal as a communion meal. But in the New Testament Jesus gives us the Eucharist in the context of the Jewish Passover meal so that, as they fed on the lamb of sacrifice, we too can feed on this new and eternal Sacrifice, the thing offered, which is His Body and Blood.

The Eucharistic Sacrifice is a participation in the Sacrifice of Calvary

What we need to recognise is that the Lamb of Sacrifice offered on Calvary is no ordinary animal; it is Christ Himself, the Victim, the only true Lamb of Sacrifice. And it is no ordinary meal since the bread and wine have been changed into His True Body and Blood. And since the things offered, bread and wine, have been modified, changed, transubstantiated into the Body and Blood of Christ, the Mass truly is a sacrifice.

As I remarked at the beginning of this chapter, the sacrificial character of the Eucharist is made clear and is manifested in the words Christ used to institute the Eucharist: "This is my body which

is given for you" and "This cup which is poured out for you is the
New Covenant in my blood."[58] In the Eucharist, Christ gives us the
same body which he surrendered for us on the cross, the same blood
which he "poured out for many for the forgiveness of sins."[59]

I also referred earlier to the Old Testament idea that there has to
be a change in the gift before it becomes a sacrifice, the removal of
the blood from the animal. But the Sacrifice of the Mass is different.
It is referred to as an 'unbloody sacrifice' because His blood once
shed does not need to be shed again. But a change has nevertheless
occurred, a far more profound change than that which characterised
Old Testament sacrifices. There is not another death, not another
shedding of blood, but the transformation, Transubstantiation of
the bread and wine into the true Body and blood of Christ.

But there is still more. Since the Eucharist is the memorial of
Christ's Passover, it is also in that sense too, a sacrifice. The Blessed
Eucharist was given to us during the Feast of the Passover, so that 'do
this in remembrance of me' is to be understood as a participation in
the sacrifice about to happen.[60] The offering of Jesus, i.e. his life, only
becomes a sacrifice with the real change effected in Him through his
death and resurrection. 'In remembrance' (Greek ἀνάμνησις) means
making present a past event, but now not just in the virtual sense of
the OT sacrifices but in a *real and actual sense.*[61]

As the *Catechism of the Catholic Church* reminds us, the Eucharist
is a making present (re-presentation) of the sacrifice of the cross
because not only is it a memorial but also because the fruits of that
sacrifice continue to be applied to all those who participate in that
offering.

> [Christ], our Lord and God, was once and for all to offer
> himself to God the Father by his death on the altar of
> the cross, to accomplish there an everlasting redemption.
> But because his priesthood was not to end with his death,

---

58 Luke 22: 19-20.
59 Matthew 26:28.
60 Luke 22:19-20. Mt 26:28.
61 1 Corinthians 10:16 and cf *Lumen Gentium* 3; cf. 1 Cor 5:7.

at the Last Supper "on the night when he was betrayed," [he wanted] to leave to his beloved spouse the Church a visible sacrifice (as the nature of man demands) by which the bloody sacrifice which he was to accomplish once for all on the cross would be re-presented, its memory perpetuated until the end of the world, and its salutary power be applied to the forgiveness of the sins we daily commit.[62]

Consequently, since we are baptised into Christ we are part of Him. Therefore through our Baptism and in the offering of the Mass we can continue to offer ourselves, our souls and bodies, as a living sacrifice though Him, with Him and in Him. We enter into the Heavenly Sanctuary through a new and living way, Jesus Christ who is both Priest and Victim, because we have been baptised into him (Hebrews 10:19ff and cf Hebrews 12:22-24). Therefore, associating ourselves with Him we can offer ourselves in union with Him because we belong to Him. As the priestly people of God (1 Peter 2:9) we join with the ministerial priest (the one ordained) who has a particular share in the priesthood of Christ, so that we can participate in the offering of all peoples, all angels, and all the saints from all time and eternity.

> To the offering of Christ are united not only the members still here on earth, but also those already *in the glory of heaven*. In communion with and commemorating the Blessed Virgin Mary and all the saints, the Church offers the Eucharistic sacrifice. In the Eucharist the Church is as it were at the foot of the cross with Mary, united with the offering and intercession of Christ.[63]

We can this do because:

a) We are baptised into Christ and belong to Him.

b) Hanging onto his 'coat tails', so to speak, we have the

---

62 Council of Trent (1562): DS 1740; cf. 1 Cor 11:23; Heb 7:24, 27; and cf CCC 1366.
63 CCC 1370.

right to enter the heavenly sanctuary to be renewed in
the worship of heaven which is the pleading of the one
all-sufficient sacrifice.

c) In union with Christ we offer ourselves to Him as the
best and only gift we have to offer, a gift made worthy by
its being associated with the offering of the God-Man,
the priest-Victim. How? Well, in baptism we were made
members of the Church which is the Body of Christ. That
being the case we can offer our lives to God the Father
because they have been made worthy to be offered. They
are worthy because living in Christ our sins are forgiven.
We have something to offer in sacrifice, ourselves in union
with Christ's sacrifice. So, since we are united with Christ
in baptism and are the Body of Christ, it follows that
in the Mass the whole Christ offers the whole Christ to
the Father, because we offer our lives in union with His
perfect offering of Himself.

d) He gives us power to live a good life because we feed
on the Victim, Jesus Himself, who returns to us our gifts
of bread and wine (symbols of ourselves) as His true and
substantially real Body and Blood. We commit ourselves
to love our fellow believers (1 Peter 2:7).

e) In the Eucharist we are reconciled both to God and to
our fellow man (Romans 14:15 and cf Colossians 3:5),
a reconciliation which can only come about because of
the reconciliation God has brought us through His death
and resurrection.

St Augustine admirably summed up this doctrine that moves us
to an ever more complete participation in our Redeemer's sacrifice
which we celebrate in the Eucharist:

> This wholly redeemed city, the assembly and society of
> the saints, is offered to God as a universal sacrifice by
> the high priest who in the form of a slave went so far
> as to offer Himself for us in His Passion, to make us

the Body of so great a head. . . . Such is the sacrifice of Christians: "we who are many are one Body in Christ". The Church continues to reproduce this sacrifice in the sacrament of the altar so well-known to believers wherein it is evident to them that in what she offers she herself is offered.[64]

So then the Sacrifice of the Mass is the Sacrifice of Christ on Calvary, a supreme act of worship in which we immerse ourselves in the means of our salvation and redemption.[65] In union with the whole Church living and departed we can offer the Holy Sacrifice for the living and the departed knowing that it will be for the benefit of their souls.

> Then, we pray [in the anaphora] for the holy fathers and bishops who have fallen asleep, and in general for all who have fallen asleep before us, in the belief that it is a great benefit to the souls on whose behalf the supplication is offered, while the holy and tremendous Victim is present. ... By offering to God our supplications for those who have fallen asleep, if they have sinned, we ... offer Christ sacrificed for the sins of all, and so render favorable, for them and for us, the God who loves man.[66]

These may be new concepts to many people but, Robert and Mads, they are accessible concepts once we have stopped to think about it for a while. And when we 'get' the ideas of sacrifice and Transubstantiation, we can really understand that the Mass is the most perfect act of worship and provided to us by the God-Man Jesus Christ. Immersed in the offering of the sacrifice of Calvary in and through the Mass, we participate in the worship of heaven together with our Blessed Lady, all the saints and martyrs, all the Christians who have gone before us, and all the angels and archangels.

At the earthly altar in our parish church, Heaven and Earth meet. We enter the heavenly sanctuary and worship at the heavenly

---

64 St. Augustine, De civ Dei, 10, 6: PL 41, 283; cf. Rom 12:5; and cf CCC 1372.
65 And cf St Thomas Aquinas, *Summa Theogica*, III, q. 83, a. 1.
66 From the *Catechism of the Catholic Church*, paragraph 1371.

altar where Christ continues to plead his sacrifice for all time and eternity. At the same time Christ becomes present for us as bread and wine are changed into his Body and Blood on the earthly altar. Transubstantiation, although a separate idea, is nevertheless needed if we are to accept what Christ taught us, that the Sacrifice of Calvary and the Sacrifice of the Mass are one and the same sacrifice. We need Christ's presence in the Eucharist because "without the Real Presence of Christ, the same event or the same action could not take place."[67] Or as Sokolowski puts it in another place, "we cannot have the one without the other; no Transubstantiation without identity of sacrifice, and no identity of sacrifice without Transubstantiation."[68]

---

67 Robert Sokolowski, "The Eucharist and Transubstantiation" published in "Notes and Comments" in *Communio* 24, 4 (Winter, 1997) 868.
68 *Ibid.*

6

The Real Presence of Christ in the Eucharist

So now Robert let me turn my attention to Transubstantiation, the teaching that the bread and wine used in the Mass are transformed into the Body and Blood of Jesus Christ. Having explained the real nature of the Mass as a Sacrifice, I am now writing this short essay in the hope that you may find such a belief intellectually credible. To do that I am going to have to start with some really fundamental things in which I know you already believe. It would be impossible for me to even begin to discuss this subject if you were an atheist! But since you have already grasped the reality of God's existence, I think I can at least give you some reasons why the Catholic belief in the Real Presence may be accepted through the synthesis of faith and reason.

I believe in God

So to begin with, we know that the whole of Christian belief rests in the first instance on the objective truth that God exists and that He is the creator of all that is and the author of all truth. You may find that set out in the *Catechism of the Catholic Church* (CCC) in paragraph 2465 and supported by the Biblical references cited there. According to Christian belief God created everything that is visible to the human eye as well as all those things which are not visible. God is, by definition, Himself uncreated. He just is. That is why we speak of God's existence in terms of "being".

Through the *miraculous* power that belongs to God alone, He called into existence everything, material as well as spiritual (e.g. the angels) as it pleased Him to do. That God is the creator of all that is, accords with sound reason, and is evident to nearly every human being. Belief in God is supported by the great arguments for the existence of God as formulated by St Thomas Aquinas. There are a number of reasonably well known arguments for the existence of God, which are not so much a proof that God exists as they are arguments which show belief in God to be reasonable and atheism unreasonable. I am referring here to the quite reasonable inference people draw when they look about them and consider how all this could have come into being and in such an ordered and harmonious way. In fact the whole of science assumes we can find the rules by which nature is governed in order that we can use natural forces for good ends. People have always called the uncreated creator of the universe, God, and have noticed the exquisite design which could only come from a supreme intelligence. But I know I don't have to argue about this belief which is shared by the overwhelming majority of human beings.

Moreover, should God withdraw his power, all that is would cease to exist since it exists only on account of the "being" and sustaining power of the one who is the Creator.

As I say, one way we have of knowing that God exists is through his creation. We look at all there is, the stars, the moon, the beauty of creation, and man himself, and we see the presence of God mediated to us. Put another way, the material world mediates to us the presence of God such that human beings, contemplating it, say together with the Psalmist: "The Lord created the heavens by his command, the sun, moon, and stars by his spoken word …. Worship the Lord, all the earth! Honour him, all peoples of the world! When he spoke, the world was created; at his command everything appeared."[69] When considering himself against the magnificence of the heavens and the earth, man is overcome at the thought that God has made him in his own image and likeness, and actually cares for human beings as individuals and as a family: "O Lord, our Lord, your greatness is seen

---

69 Ps 33: 6, 8.

in all the world! ... When I look at the sky, which you have made, at the moon and the stars, which you set in their places – what is man, that you think of him; mere man that you care for him?"[70]

While human beings find it difficult to conceptualise the God who cannot be seen,[71] nevertheless it is characteristic of human beings to recognise the God they cannot see but can 'feel' spiritually and emotionally. Moreover, reason teaches man to believe in the Creator God because such a belief is the only truly reasonable explanation for the world as we humans experience it to be. Atheism is unreasonable and does not accord with man's deepest intuitions. In the end man believes not only that God exists but comes to believe in Him because He can be known personally. That is to say, man comes to have *Faith* in God. "To have faith is to be sure of the things we hope for, to be certain of the things we cannot see."[72] Put another way, there is something within us that draws us to the God we cannot see, because God has made us dependent on Him. It would indeed be odd if God expects us to know Him and to love Him and yet has made us to be spiritually inert and insensitive to Him in whose presence we live and upon whom we depend for life itself.

Human Beings as mediators of God's presence in the world

Human beings themselves mediate the presence of God to each other. We see Him in each other and become aware that human beings cannot simply be accounted for in terms of molecules, genes, and chemicals. Our reverence for human life is predicated on us seeing "more" in human beings than in any other kind of being or inanimate thing. Whenever we are tempted to think of human beings as just another animal, more or less valuable depending upon race, ability, beauty, or some other extrinsic factor, we fail to see the real beauty and dignity of the human being. Yet human beings do see that there is an intrinsic or inherent dignity in the human being no matter that

70 Ps 8:1, 3-4.
71 John 1:18.
72 Hebrews: 11:1.

some atheists do not. For example, the whole world has signed on to the Charter of the UN which in its documents insists on the inherent dignity of the human being and the fundamental rights which derive from that human dignity. (cf Universal Declaration on Human Rights of 1948 and the International Covenant on Civil and Political Rights 1966) Moreover, the very word animate, to describe living beings, is derived from the Latin word *anima* which means soul.

Human beings can also, through what they create, mediate beauty and a sense of the transcendent. Mozart's music cannot be simply accounted for in physical terms, sound, wave patterns and so on. No, the way that the music has been crafted by the musician is meant to communicate to us something beyond the sounds themselves such that the sounds themselves are intimately and irremediably connected with the truths they signify. A beautiful Mass setting fit for the purpose of worshipping God is one that in and of itself conveys to us a sense of the transcendent that takes us from where we are now into the heavenly sanctuary, into the presence of God Himself. The same is true of beautiful religious poetry, the language of the Mass, and so on. The magnificent churches and cathedrals designed and built by human beings convey in and through them something of the reality and the mystery of God.

Why do we value and respect paintings and photographs of loved ones? The answer to that question is, I believe, because the painting of a person, and even a photograph, has 'something' of the person within it. This is why photographs of loved ones are kept and protected, an assault on the image being seen somehow as an assault on that person. The national flag is treated with respect because it too, in some metaphysical sense, is more than cloth and image but contains something of the nation which it represents.

God mediates Himself to us by becoming a man

Given our belief in God as the creator of all that is, and that he mediates his presence to us through material things, including ourselves, we note that God became a man in order that we might be able to see Him, relate to Him, and know Him as he really is.

Jesus said, "He who has seen me has seen the Father."[73] The point about the incarnation is that in Jesus we have One who is fully God and fully a human being. This idea is expressed in the term which describes Mary as *Theotokos*. That is, Mary is the Mother of God. Mary is the Mother (relationship of human flesh) of Christ, which is to say that he is fully human, conceived and nurtured within His mother's womb. She is the Mother of God, which is to say that the one conceived in her is God, the Second Person of the Trinity. Here we have the fundamental sacramental principle writ large, an animate material being, Jesus the man, is also God himself. So, through the material order God is fully manifested to us in a man. It is therefore not idolatrous to worship Christ because He is fully God as well as fully a human being. Jesus is the Word referred to in the first chapter of St John's Gospel, the Word who was active in the creation of the world,[74] the Word who became flesh[75] and came among us, full of grace and truth.

Responding to scepticism about Jesus

Sceptics looked at Jesus and said, "He's a man, he's just a man".[76] How could God who is infinite be conveyed to us in finite human flesh? For the sceptic the visible is all there is; the finite cannot contain the infinite. The very idea of God coming to us in finite human form is an absurdity. The resurrection is regarded as an absurdity.[77] BUT … to take that view is to relapse into a form of practical atheism because it presupposes that God is not capable of doing what seems impossible to the finite human brain. The creation of the universe *ex nihilo* (out of nothing) is also beyond human comprehension as is God Himself. Yet we human beings know on the basis of sound reason and spiritual experience that God does exist, and that the existence of the universe without the God who designed it is unreasonable and renders life meaningless.

73 cf John 8: 19; John 14: 8-14.
74 John 1:1-5.
75 John 1:14.
76 cf Mark 6:1-6.
77 Acts 17:16-32.

The truth of this doctrine of Christ, that He is at once fully and truly God and man, is itself built on the miracle of the resurrection, the evidences for which are historically available. These evidences include eye witness accounts. That the eye witnesses are reliable may be seen from the radical change that the resurrection made to their lives. That they really believed what they saw, heard, and felt, is also evidenced by the fact that they were prepared to die for this truth. Why would you put yourself at risk of martyrdom if Christ did not rise from the dead and that, accordingly, as far as you know, this is the only life to be had? Moreover, there were very many eye witnesses, an empty tomb and no other verifiable account of what happened to the body.

The resurrection affirms that Jesus is who he says he is. He is God. A further evidence is the living faith of a billion Catholics today, and the billions that have lived since the time of Christ, a faith which is predicated upon a living relationship with Christ who is alive and not dead in some final sense of dead and therefore no longer accessible to our senses. If Jesus really is who he says he is, that is if he really is God come among us, then what he discloses to us about the nature of God is infallibly true.

Christ and the Eucharist

So when Jesus taught that we have to eat his body and drink his blood[78] we have to take it that he meant what he said. But Jesus would not ask us to do that in a way that would be disgusting to us, eating flesh and drinking blood in a purely carnal sense. For a whole raft of reasons connected with the Passover celebration (discussed in the previous chapter) he gave us bread and wine which, he said, would be, at His Word, his body and blood which we should take, eat and drink.

If a person believes that Jesus is God, then that person must take Jesus at his word, so that when we do as he commands the bread and wine are changed into his true body and blood. The problems that remain are these: In what sense are we to believe that the Host is the

---

78 See in particular John 6: 25-70.

Body of Jesus? How can we affirm what our senses seem to deny? Is the change of the bread and wine into the body and blood of Christ something that can be explained naturalistically or is it a miracle, a miracle which occurs each and every time the priest celebrates the Sacrifice of the Mass?

In a moment I will deal with each of these questions in order:

1. In what sense are we to believe that the Host is the Body of Jesus?
2. How can we affirm what our senses seem to deny?
3. Is the change of the bread and wine into the body and blood of Christ something that can be explained naturalistically or is it a miracle, a miracle which occurs each and every time the priest celebrates the Sacrifice of the Mass?

The necessity of Faith

Before attempting to clarify the important intellectual questions I want to suggest to you Robert that, as St Augustine taught us, "faith precedes understanding", that "I believe in order to understand". This is an approach we take to most of the really important things in life.

Take for example the relationship between a man and a woman that leads to marriage. Increasingly love requires us to have faith in the one we love. And in having faith in him or her we discover so much more to that person than we could ever have imagined. There are good reasons why we have faith in the one we love, reasons which have to do with our already felt experience of that person, who she is and what she shows of herself. Yet, in the end, to come to a deeper and deeper knowledge and appreciation of her I have to commit myself to her in marriage.

Scientists have faith in the scientific method. There are certain logical problems in using the scientific method to prove the scientific method. But on the basis of experience we trust the method or methods and explore the mysteries of nature. And our understanding of nature is increased a thousand fold.

So it is with the mystery of the Eucharist. We trust that Jesus, who is God, will be true to His word, and then we allow ourselves to be drawn into the mystery of the Eucharist finding that our belief in the Real Presence is justified by our spiritual experience, and our understanding of what that means is deepened.

I believe in order to understand.

When a desperate man brought his seriously ill child to Jesus for a cure he asked Jesus "if you can do anything, have pity on us and help us." Jesus' response: "If you can? All things are possible to him who believes." The man responds with an act of faith, "I believe; help my unbelief". And the child recovered.

When we believe in the Real Presence solely on account of the promise of the God/Man Jesus, we are then free to use wisdom to ponder the depths of this miracle, this mystery which Christ uses to draw us to himself.

So let us now go to the intellectual issues at hand. Bear with me, Robert and Mads. I believe that people in their 20s are more than able to follow a good technical argument. And what follows is not a *proof* that belief in the Real Presence is true, but a process of philosophical reasoning that can help us see that such a belief, such an act of faith, is consistent with human reason. Reason by itself can never prove the mysterious and miraculous events that occur, events which God causes to happen by an act of his sovereign power. We need the support of other faculties, such as faith, to bring us to that sureness of the things we hope for, the certainty of the things we cannot see

In what sense is the Host the Body of Christ?

Since the Church believes that Jesus is God, she begins by accepting the truth of what Christ taught, i.e. "This is my body", "This is my blood", "unless you eat my flesh and drink my blood you will have no life in you". But what does this mean?

The presence is clearly not a crudely physical presence since the bread and wine remain bread and wine to the senses of taste, touch, feel and smell.

The presence must then be a metaphysical presence but nonetheless real and substantial.

We need also to keep in mind that the body of Christ is no longer the body seen by the Disciples and others prior to the resurrection since that body no longer exists. The resurrected body is qualitatively different in that Christ could appear and disappear, appear to different people at the same time, was not bound by space and time, could move through walls, and so on. Thus we know that the resurrected and glorified body of Christ has qualities which are very different from the qualities of our bodies and is less restricted, qualities which we will enjoy when we, too, participate in the resurrection.

Therefore the real presence of Christ in the Eucharist must satisfy a number of different criteria:

1. The presence is metaphysical and not physical in a carnal or fleshly sense
2. The Christ present is the resurrected Christ, there being no other[79]
3. The presence of Christ must nonetheless be real and substantial to satisfy the criterion that it is really and truly his body and blood.

The Church uses the term transubstantiation as a means of identifying what this change means. Transubstantiation does not explain *how* the change occurs. It serves to show its consistency with sound reason. It is based upon the metaphysics of Aristotle.

Metaphysics is the science of real as distinguished from phenomenal being. It makes a distinction between the way a thing appears to be from a purely physical point of view, and what it is in reality. For example, there is more to bread than simply its appearances or characteristics, characteristics which may be the same as or similar to characteristics of another thing. But bread has a particular identity as bread as distinct from a croissant or pasta. This Aristotle described

---

79 Cf Robert Sokolowski, "The Eucharist and Transubstantiation" in Notes and Comments" in *Communio* 24, 4 (Winter, 1997) 870. "The bread and wine of the Eucharist become the body and blood of the Lord, but they become specifically his resurrected and glorified body and blood."

as its essential reality.

Without going into a detailed understanding of metaphysics we see that a thing, such as bread, has what Aristotle calls its *accidents*, that is, those aspects of bread which are apprehended by the senses of taste, touch, feel, and smell, and its *substance* or *identity*, the breadiness of the bread if you will. The *substance* of the bread is a spiritual or metaphysical reality, not physical as with the *accidents*. In the same way a human being is a dynamic unity of body and soul, the body being your accidents and the soul being your *metaphysical* or *spiritual identity*, your *substance*, who you really are.

Of course the body is not separable from the soul with the soul as a kind of motor under the bonnet of the car. The body and soul are a dynamic unity such that if one touches the body of a person one is in a real sense touching that person's soul or identity. This is one reason why we protect ourselves against unwanted touches because touch of itself is an intimacy.

So, the doctrine of transubstantiation tells us that at the command of Christ and through the power of the Holy Spirit acting through the priest who stands in *persona Christi*, the substance of the bread and the wine is changed into the substance of the body and blood of Christ. This is not merely symbolic. It is a real change so that the Eucharistic elements convey Christ to us, really, truly, and substantially. That is, it is no longer really bread but the Body of Christ despite what our senses seem to convey to us.

How can we affirm what our senses seem to deny?

If we consider the case of identical twins, we have before us two human beings who are physically identical even down to their genes. Let us call them Jim and John. We may think we are talking to Jim, yet we are really talking to John. That is, our physical senses have limitations when it comes to determining the real identity of the one we are talking to; same bodily characteristics, physically speaking, yet two different identities.

So, at one level we may think the bread of the Eucharist is no different from any other piece of unleavened bread. But in reality, and through faith, we apprehend that this is no ordinary bread. On the contrary its real identity is Jesus Himself.

St Thomas Aquinas, following Aristotle provides the best insights into the meaning of transubstantiation. He begins with the distinction between *substance* and *accidents* when he refers to things. *Accidents* are those aspects of a thing which are apprehended by our senses of touch, feel, and smell. So *accidents* are the properties of a thing which can as well exist in some other thing or be used to describe some other thing. Colour, for example, is an *accident*. You can have a white wall, a white person, a white building or a white ball. *Substance*, on the other hand is what does not exist in another thing nor can it be said of another. Aristotle is Aristotle and his identity or *substance* cannot be ascribed to another. It is the same as identical twins to which I have already made reference. Jim is Jim and John is John.

Now normally the *substance* supports the *accidents*. Bread, for example, has all the properties of bread, properties each of which could be ascribed to some other thing. But the real identity of the bread is in the metaphysical reality which we call its *substance*. The physical sciences cannot examine the metaphysical. Those sciences are limited to an examination of the accidents only, and have no account of substance. But through philosophy we recognise there is more to reality than the accidents. The human soul, for example is a metaphysical reality which gives that particular human being his or her own reality as distinct from any other human being no matter how similar (even identical) his or her own accidents may appear.

In the case of transubstantiation, the substances of the bread and wine are each changed into the substance of the body and blood of Christ. Here the accidents give the lie to the reality actually present because a miracle has occurred whereby the accidents are supported by another substance, it invariably being the case that the substance and the accidents cannot be distilled from each other, anymore than the soul can be distilled from the body.

The problem that remains is this: if in nature the accidents are not independent of the substance, how can the accidents of bread and wine remain unsupported by the substances of bread and wine since it has been replaced by the substances of Christ's true body and blood? Although some might say that the substance of Christ's body would now serve that purpose that is simply not possible according to Aquinas. This is so "because the substance of the human body cannot in any way be affected by such accidents; nor is it possible for Christ's body, now that it is transfigured and cannot suffer any more, to be altered so as to receive these qualities."[80]

So it is, according to St Thomas, that the accidents, the species itself remains but without a subject to support those accidents. This, too, is part of the miracle of transubstantiation. We really experience the accidents of bread and wine in terms of touch, feel, smell etc, but actually receive the subject of the consecrated bread which is not the substance of bread but Christ Himself, the true subject of the transubstantiated bread. And since God is the first cause of all that is, by His power He can sustain the accidents of bread and wine even though it no longer has its proper cause, the substance of bread.[81]

Here grace builds on nature but does not destroy or disfigure it. David Berger puts it this way:

> The supernatural separation of substance and accident is neither logically contradictory nor inherently impossible, as the definition of the accident merely includes the claim to an actualized existence in the substance, not the claim to existence itself. This natural claim remains intact even after the supernatural conversion of the essence.[82]

Is the change of the bread and wine into the body and blood of Christ something that can be explained naturalistically or is it a miracle, a miracle which occurs each and every time the priest celebrates the Sacrifice of the Mass?

The change of the substance of bread into the substance of Jesus cannot be explained naturalistically because it is an event which

---

80 St Thomas Aquinas, *Summa Theologiae* III, q. 77, a. 1 and cited in David Berger, *Thomas Aquinas & The Liturgy*, Ann Arbor: Sapientia Press 2005, 106-107.
81 *Ibid.*
82 David Berger, *ibid.*, 107-108 and cf P Sedlmayr, "Die Lehre des hl. Thomas von den accidentia sine subjecto remanentia", *Divus Thomas* (F) 12 (1934), 315-326.

occurs through the sovereign power of God who is not limited by the physical laws of nature, laws of which He Himself is the author. The acceptance of this miracle by the faithful is because of their faith in God, in Jesus Christ who is the Son of God and whose Word may be trusted, and because it is not contrary to reason. The consecration of bread and wine in the Mass is a miracle, a daily miracle which takes place on altars all around the world. In the miracle of the Mass, the priest, acting as Christ, using the powers conferred on him at ordination and above all though the power of the Holy Spirit upon whom we call during the Eucharistic prayer, causes the transubstantiation of bread and wine.

St John Chrysostom ('Golden mouth', AD 345 - 407) puts it this way: "It is not man that causes the things offered to become the Body and Blood of Christ, but he who was crucified for us, Christ himself. The priest in the role of Christ pronounces these words, but their power and grace is God's. This is my body, he says. The word transforms the things offered."[83]

Christ is truly present as he promised.

How then can we apprehend his Real Presence?

If the presence of Christ is not physical in the sense that the accidents too are converted, i.e. the bread and wine remain bread and wine as far as the senses are concerned, then how can we experience the real Presence of Christ in the Most Holy Sacrament of the Altar? St Thomas Aquinas says that this is something that "cannot be apprehended by the senses, but *only by faith*, which relies on divine authority." St Cyril of Alexandria (AD 376–444) says: "Do not doubt whether this is true, but rather receive the words of the Saviour in faith, for since he is the truth, he cannot lie."[84]

As I recalled earlier in this short essay, "To have faith is to be sure of the things we hope for, to be certain of the things we cannot see."[85] The good reason for believing that the bread and wine are changed into the Body and Blood of Christ is that Jesus, Himself

---

83 St John Chrysostom, *De proditione. Judae.* 1:6.
84 *In Lucam* 22, 19.
85 Hebrews: 11:1.

fully God as well as fully Man, said so. The authority for this belief
is Divine authority. By faith we apprehend the truth of what he said.
And since 'faith precedes understanding', 'I believe in order that I may
understand', we come to the Eucharist with faith and discover the
truth through our own experience of worship, prayer, and devotion.
Through the eyes of faith we see him on the altar and in receiving
Holy Communion we take Him into ourselves, His soul, His body,
and his Divinity, and in our lives we experience the truth of that
Holy Communion as our lives become transformed by the grace and
power of this wonderful sacrament.

> Godhead here in hiding, whom I do adore
> Masked by these bare shadows, shape and nothing more,
> See, Lord, at thy service low lies here a heart
> Lost, all lost in wonder at the God thou art.
> Seeing, touching, tasting are in thee deceived;
> How says trusty hearing? That shall be believed;
> What God's Son has told me, take for truth do I;
> Truth himself speaks truly or there's nothing true.

This hymn written by St Thomas (*Adoro te*) concludes by saying
that if Jesus, who is "the Way, the Truth, and the Life"[86], is lying,
then nothing is true!

And St Ambrose (AD 340-97) poses this question: "could not
Christ's word which can make from nothing what did not exist, change
existing things into what they were not before? It is no less a feat to
give things their original nature than to change their nature."[87]

Psychological and emotional responses

So, Robert and Mads, when I come into the "presence" of Christ in
the Blessed Sacrament, how do I feel? Well, it all depends.

When you meet a person for the first time, you may see not much
more than the outward appearance of that person, the way that person
seems to be. For various reasons outward appearances might make

---

86 John 14: 6.
87 St Ambrose, *De mysteriis.* 9, 52.

such an impact that we are sidetracked by that. But the more we spend time with that person the more we see beyond the "accidents", so to speak, to the real person who is present and mediated to us through those outward signs.

To begin with that may make a very deep and lasting impression, an impression which may fade the more we get used to being in his or her company. Familiarity. But that doesn't mean to say we love or admire them less. Indeed, and especially where a spouse is concerned, that familiarity, far from breeding contempt, may lead to such an easiness of feeling, such a deep love, that it is a love beyond mere superficial 'romanticism'.

It is the same with the Blessed Sacrament. When one first sees beyond the accidents of bread to the reality of Christ's presence one may feel completely overwhelmed, a deep sense of being in love with Christ with whom one has a personal relationship. Over time, we may become familiar with being with Him and, if we are careful as we should be, that familiarity can become the basis of a deeper love for Christ which is less dependent upon more ephemeral but deeply felt emotional feelings.

All relationships have to be worked on. That applies to the husband/wife relationship, and to all deep personal friendships. When we don't see people enough, spend enough time with them, friendships can fade. So it is with our relationship with Christ. For His part Christ is always available to us. Mass is offered every day. The Sacrament is reserved in Churches for the purposes of prayer and adoration as well as being there for the sick and debilitated. If we want to develop our relationship with Christ in the Most Holy Sacrament of the Altar we should try to go to Mass as often as possible and at least on every Sunday and Holy Day of Obligation which is our minimum duty. And the more often we come to Him, the deeper our friendship with Him is developed. He is always there for us. Are we always there for Him?

So, feelings? It all depends on what you mean and the state of mind you happen to be in at the time. What is true for all other relationships is also true in our relationship with Christ. So never be

discouraged if at times you seem to 'feel' nothing. Just being with
Him can be enough on those occasions to see you through.

So Robert and Mads I hope I have said enough for you to see
why it is reasonable to believe in the miracle of transubstantiation.
There is no scientific 'proof' available for a metaphysical reality
which can only really be apprehended through the eyes of faith.
But it is reasonable, not only not contrary to reason to so believe,
but completely consonant with sound reason to accept what faith
reveals.

> I believe in order to understand, said St Augustine. If
> we accept Christ at his word we will discover the truth
> of his real presence and find sufficient understanding to
> give confidence in that belief.
>
> Blessed, Praised, and Hallowed be Jesus Christ on His
> Throne of Glory, and in the Most Holy Sacrament of
> the Altar. Amen and Amen.

7
Conclusion

The best religious decisions I have made in my life were my decisions, when I was young, to embrace the Christian Faith and build my relationship with Jesus Christ, and much later to seek full communion with the Catholic Church. I have also been blessed to have been an Anglican priest for 17 years and a Catholic priest since the 20 May 1995.

In that time I have met and known many fine priests both Anglican and Catholic. Archbishop Thomas Thornton Reed who ordained me an Anglican priest in 1970 was a scholar, a gentleman, orthodox Christian, and, later, a friend. I admired him greatly. Archbishop Leonard Faulkner ordained me as a Catholic priest in 1995. His pastoral care and sensitivity to my position were outstanding and I will never forget him. Monsignor Robert Aitken and Monsignor Robert Egar, two Adelaide Diocesan priests and former Vicars General, provided outstanding support and care.

Although Alison and I have been through some very difficult times together because of our decision to seek full communion with the Catholic Church, I can honestly say that God has cared for us and provided.

My love and concern for Anglicans has always remained. After all, it was the Anglican Church that first introduced me to the Catholic Faith. The next chapter in this book contains an account of my role in assisting the Traditional Anglican Communion make its historically significant unconditional request to the Holy See for Full Corporate Union with the Catholic Church.

This book is not an autobiography. It is the story of one person's religious journey and his involvement with others who, too, have been attracted to the Catholic Church. Nor, indeed, is it in any way meant to suggest any particular virtue in the author but, rather, despite all his weaknesses and sinfulness, a testimony to the way God seeks us out and continues to call us all into the fullness of truth which is only to be found in the Catholic Church.

I have found spiritual fulfilment in the Catholic Church. The Mass really is the "source and summit of the Christian life"[88]. It was the Mass that converted me from scepticism and agnosticism to a living relationship with Jesus. And it was the Mass which in turn led me to the priesthood of the Anglican Church. The necessity for authenticity and validity redirected my attention back to the question of authority, and to a reconsideration of the constitution of the Church as given to the Apostles by Christ. In all of this I have discerned the power of the Holy Spirit to prompt, inspire and guide me to the Truth once revealed in Jesus, the Gospel of Salvation. And it is the Catholic Church, the true Church of Jesus Christ, which has preserved the Gospel of Jesus in all its fullness.

If you truly love our Lord Jesus Christ then you must also love His Mother. He gave Mary to us as our Mother too. She is the Holy and Ever-Virgin Mother of God, Mother of the Church, Mother of all Christians, Queen of Heaven and Queen of the Most Holy Rosary. She conceived in her womb the Man-God Jesus through the power of the Holy Spirit, having been prepared by the Holy Spirit to accept her unique role in the scheme of salvation. What gratitude she evokes in us as we consider her heroic self-denial and obedience to the Word of God. How powerful her prayers of intercession and her example as she always directs our attention back to the God who made her and all mankind, and to her Son, our Saviour and Redeemer, our only Mediator and Advocate.

If I have been on a spiritual journey then of necessity I have also been on an intellectual journey. Enlightened by the Light of Christ and guided by the Holy Spirit, I came to embrace, while still an Anglican, the fullness of the Catholic moral tradition with all

---

88 *Lumen Gentium*, n 11 and cited in the *Catechism of the Catholic Church*, n 1324.

its subtleties and nuances. This in turn, together with my interest in bioethics, prepared the way for me to become the foundation Director of Southern Cross Bioethics Institute in Adelaide, South Australia (1987-2004), and then (2004-2009) Foundation President of Campion College Australia, Australia's first Catholic Liberal Arts tertiary institution.

At Campion I have met many outstanding Catholics: benefactors, members of the Campion Institute Board and Campion Foundation Board, academic and administrative staff, as well as students. Here we have an authentically Catholic tertiary institution in which both staff and students take the Catholic Faith very seriously and are able to live it out in the most natural way possible. It is at Campion that, despite all the difficulties involved in setting up a new tertiary institution, that I found the opportunity to express myself most fully..

Who would have predicted that God the Holy Spirit, who led me into the Catholic Church, protected me and my family in our darkest days through the goodness of so many people, Catholic priests and particularly those laymen associated with Southern Cross Care SA Inc., would have given me the opportunity to be the Foundation President of Campion College? I have received far more than I have ever given.

To God be the Glory!

And, in the end ...

You might like to know that Robert is now a Catholic. He was recently baptised, confirmed, and received his First Holy Communion. Now sharing the same Catholic Faith, Robert and Mads were married four weeks later.

8

The Traditional Anglican Communion and Full Corporate reunion with the Holy See

by Father John Fleming and Archbishop John Hepworth,
Primate of the Traditional Anglican Communion

Father John Fleming begins the story

Some people have imagined that, in becoming a Catholic in 1987, I rejected my Anglican formation and heritage in its entirety, that I no longer have any real affection for the Anglican Church and for Anglicanism generally, and that I am no longer interested in the ecumenical possibilities between Anglicanism and the Holy See. I know this because these things have been suggested to me by various people over the last 21 years since Alison and I were received into full communion with the Catholic Church.

None of these imaginings are in any way correct. I owe the fact that I am a Christian to the Anglican Church in which I was brought up. Moreover, it was Anglicanism that introduced me to the Catholic Faith, especially that part of Anglicanism to which I was attached. The Oxford Movement, inaugurated in Oxford (UK) by some of the most famous Anglican priests of the nineteenth century[89], reintroduced

---

89 John Keble's famous assize sermon on "national apostasy" in 1833 is generally reckoned as the beginning of the Oxford Movement. But its most famous and influential advocate was the John Henry Newman who was later to become a Catholic, a Catholic Priest, a Cardinal, and in 1991 proclaimed as Venerable. The Movement later became known as the Tractarian Movement because of the numerous Tracts written by Newman to assist Anglicans to rediscover their Catholic roots.

members of the Church of England to their pre-Reformation past. The Anglo-Catholic movement, as it was later called, was committed to helping Anglicans rediscover their Catholic roots, and to seeking reunion with Rome.

So it was that my Anglican formation greatly assisted me to discover the truths of Catholicism, the centrality of the Mass in the Christian life, and its other practices including auricular confession, the Rosary, Stations of the Cross and Benediction. Far from rejecting my former co-religionists I continue to maintain close friendships with many Anglicans and long for them to have what I have, the fullness of the Catholic Faith which can only be experienced in a Church in full communion with the Bishop of Rome. Especially important to me are those traditional Anglicans who want to maintain their Anglican cultural and liturgical identity but have no truck with aberrant Anglican innovations such as the ordination of women. Many of these traditional Anglicans are deeply hurt by developments in the Church of their birth and find it increasingly difficult to remain within mainstream Anglicanism.

The Traditional Anglican Communion

For me, the Traditional Anglican Communion (TAC) consisting of some 400,000 Anglican people worldwide, is the most impressive body of "Continuing Anglicans", that is Anglicans who wish to go on practising the Faith as they always have. It is impressive because it has formed ecclesial structures with clear lines of authority and so exists as a coherent organised ecclesial community. The vast majority of these people are Christians nurtured in Anglo-Catholicism. Accordingly, they wanted conversations to go on with Rome on the original agreed basis and were conscious of the damage done to those conversations by the unilateral decision of large parts of the Anglican Communion to ordain women. Put another way, they are really serious about pursuing an ecumenical rapprochement with the Holy See. But how were they to proceed? After all they are a minority of the world's Anglicans. Would they be taken seriously? Or would Rome consider them to be too small a group with which to negotiate given the existing official conversations with the Anglican Communion?

We need to remember that many of these Anglican people, in many different countries around the world, felt so excluded by the mainstream Communion that they believed, as a matter of sincere conscience, that they should seek the sacraments outside of the authority of the local bishop and the official Anglican Communion. Indeed, the TAC has expressly said that it "exists only where there is a breakdown of sacramental life and order that endangers the spiritual welfare of faithful people. It has a firm policy of waiting until there is a locally expressed need that cannot be met by provisions made for conscience by local Anglican churches. Very few Anglican provinces have made such provision."[90]

With similar "splits" occurring in different countries, the bishops representing these churches of the "Anglican Diaspora", as they termed it, met in Victoria, British Columbia in 1990. There they agreed to a Concordat which established the Traditional Anglican Communion (TAC) as a worldwide body.

The striking thing about this newly formed TAC is that it established a single College of Bishops of a single communion of local and regional churches. This ecclesiastical institution, which forms part of their Concordat, marks the TAC as something new given current Anglican arrangements which leave local churches with their own authority to decide on matters of faith and morals. Local churches, according to the Concordat, are not free

> … to derogate from Holy Scripture, or to determine unilaterally any question of Faith or Order, the authority for determining such residing in the College of Bishops of this Communion acting with such competent advice as may be available to it.[91]

The effect of this structure is to protect members of the TAC from the arbitrary decisions made by local churches which had devastated so many Anglicans, and also to provide a basis for ecumenical dialogue whereby the bishops of the TAC knew that

---

90 From a letter sent by the bishops of the TAC to the Sacred Congregation for the Doctrine of the Faith, and dated the 5th October 2007.
91 *Concordat*, 3.4.

they had authority to make the necessary decisions.

The original group of bishops who attended the meeting in Victoria, British Columbia, represented groups of Anglicans from Australia, Canada, Guatemala, and the United States. The first addition to the TAC following the ratification of the Concordat was a substantial part of the historic Anglican Church of India (consisting of bishops, clergy and people who had refused to join the Churches of North and South India in order to maintain an authentic sacramental life).

The first meeting between the TAC and Rome was held in 1991 by invitation of the Pontifical Council for Promoting Christian Unity. The founding Primate, Archbishop Louis Falk led the TAC delegation accompanied by, among others, Father John Hepworth who was subsequently elected Primate in succession to him. They met with Archbishop Pierre Duprey who, at the end of the consultation, gave this advice: "You must learn to grow and show that you can grow; you must show us that you can develop good relationships with the local Catholic Church in the places where you both co-exist; and I beg you to not needlessly amplify your episcopate".

The TAC accepted that advice and sought to implement it. Warm and practical relationships developed at the personal and parochial level in many places. The Servants of the Sacred Cross, a religious institute for women, approved by the Holy See, with both Traditional Anglican and Roman Catholic women members, has grown strongly and spread from North America to Australia. Other Institutes of Dedicated Life, reflecting the traditions of Anglican history, have been founded and grown with Roman Catholic co-operation and encouragement. TAC ordinands have, in some places, been able to complete theological studies at Catholic Universities and theological institutes. Friendships have grown between TAC bishops and Catholic bishops.

The TAC has provinces, dioceses, parishes and missionary districts worldwide, and reports a presence in Canada, the United States, Puerto Rico, Guatemala, India, Pakistan, Japan, Australia, New Zealand, the Torres Strait, Great Britain, Ireland, several European

countries, South Africa (including a substantial part of the Order
of Ethiopia – the Church of Umzi Wase Tiyopiya), Zimbabwe,
Botswana, Mozambique, Zambia, Kenya, DR Congo Cameroon, El
Salvador, Columbia and Argentina.

Reviving a stalled process

In the period between that first meeting and 2005 ecumenical progress
between the TAC and the Catholic Church seemed to stall. The TAC
continued to make approaches to the Holy See about the possibility
of reunion with the Catholic Church. But those approaches were not
always well received by the Council for Christian Unity who were
more interested in their conversations with the official Anglican
Communion under the Archbishop of Canterbury. And it was this
dicastery[92] that had to be dealt with if ecumenical discussions were
to take place. The prevailing wisdom in the Council appeared to be
informed by the belief that the wider ecumenical progress with the
Anglican Communion would be compromised if the TAC were taken
too seriously. This considerable hesitation on the part of the Vatican
in dealing with Anglican splinter groups was further enhanced by
the appointment of Rowan Williams as Archbishop of Canterbury.
Archbishop Williams was well connected with Cardinal Kasper which
probably led to an increased optimism that the ecumenical process
with Anglicans could be brought back on track. Added to this was
the Council's real uncertainty as to the provenance, legitimacy, and
stability of continuing Anglican Churches.

By late 2005 the TAC was becoming increasingly concerned
about the poor reception its ecumenical initiatives were receiving in
Rome. It seemed to the leaders of the TAC that their sincere efforts
to open a meaningful ecumenical dialogue with Rome were unlikely
to succeed.

Archbishop Hepworth, Primate of the TAC, sought a meeting
with me which was held on the 28 December 2005. It was a luncheon

---

92 Dicastery is a department of the Roman Curia, the governing body of the Vatican
responsible to the Pope. It comes from the Greek δικαστήριον, law-court, from δικάστης,
judge/juror.

meeting, held at Liana's Restaurant, Church Street, Parramatta. Also present was one of his bishops, Bishop David Chislett. Over lunch they explained to me the nature of the initiatives they had been taking, all of which were meant to initiate a serious dialogue with Rome leading to full corporate union. And they also told me how unsuccessful their attempts had been.

They explained that they were seeking my advice because of my Anglican background, my present situation as a Catholic priest, and because they thought that I might have some insights in how best to proceed and with whom.

The Fleming Response

Since my advice was being directly sought, I abandoned caution and said what I really thought. I urged the bishops to abandon current approaches based upon 'ecumenical dialogue'. These approaches involved theological commissions talking for years about the theological differences between the two sides, and trying to find a form of words to which both sides could agree. And since the theologians have no real authority, what they agree to has to be then reviewed by those who have the real authority in matters of faith and morals. It was my belief that the TAC was in a very different place theologically from the Anglican Communion and well situated to cut to the chase. I suggested that if the TAC was really serious about its future and about full corporate reunion with Rome as an integral part of that future they needed to take a whole new approach. This approach was outlined by me as follows:

> 1. That the TAC seeks corporate reunion with the Holy See without condition. In this way there would be no need for committees discussing doctrine and reporting back to various authorities. It would be a straight out application for corporate reunion, no strings attached.
> 2. To achieve point 1 above, local synods of the TAC should be asked to consider, and if thought fit, pass motions to the effect that there now no longer exist any

doctrinal or moral differences between the teaching of the TAC and the Catholic Church.

3. Any petition to Rome would need to include an explicit recognition of the Petrine Office (i.e. the Office of Pope) as being of the *esse* of the Church. Put simply it would mean that the TAC accepts that the constitution of the Church as given by Christ included the leadership of St Peter as it has been handed on in the Church ever since. That the Pope has real and immediate jurisdiction in every local Church and enjoys the gift of infallibility when teaching in certain circumstances. There would need also to be an acceptance of the proposition that the Church founded by Jesus Christ and committed to the care of St Peter most perfectly subsists in the Catholic Church with the Pope, the Bishop of Rome, being the legitimate successor of St Peter. The Pope and bishops in communion with him have the task of governing the Church.

4. The TAC would also need to make it clear to Rome that it fully understands that the question of Holy Orders in the TAC would need to be addressed, and that the TAC would accept whatever the Catholic Church required to be done to assure validity, including the possibility that its ministers would need to be re-ordained.

5. If the TAC really wanted to give clear and unmistakable evidence of the seriousness of its ecumenical intentions it could do so by a clear sign that it accepted all of the teachings to be found in the *Catechism of the Catholic Church*. In other words, TAC bishops signing a copy of the *Catechism* would put beyond doubt doctrinal issues leaving the way open for a discussion on just how the TAC might be fully incorporated into the Catholic Church with the TAC being ready to accept the guidance of the Holy See.

This approach was radically different from previous TAC

policy. But knowing good Anglo-Catholics as I do, and Archbishop Hepworth as I do, and wanting only what I thought would offer the TAC its best chance of fulfilling its historic role, I was bold enough to make these proposals. We also discussed the need for members of the TAC to be able to maintain their cultural and liturgical distinctiveness, and a real sense of continuity of identity as it entered into full communion with the Catholic Church. Moreover, I was confident that if Archbishop Hepworth accepted my proposals he had all of the necessary personal, intellectual, and leadership skills to see it through whatever the personal cost to himself.

In the event, Archbishop Hepworth and Bishop Chislett accepted my proposals in their entirety and the Archbishop further accepted that it was his role to persuade the TAC of the importance of this process. By 2006 he had successfully secured agreement to this process by votes of Synods in Australia, US, Canada, England, South Africa, and India. His outstanding work came to a major climax on the 5 October 2007 when the Bishops and Vicars General of the TAC signed a letter to the Holy See seeking full corporate reunion with the Holy See. The Archbishop will explain how that came to be and what it all means.

Archbishop John Hepworth, Primate of the TAC, takes up the story:

I had known Father Fleming for long enough to trust both his insights into Catholicism and his adroit political skills. As his honorary assistant priest in his final Anglican parish, I watched his very real agonising with his conscience as he left behind the church of his upbringing and journeyed into the Catholic Church. I had watched for years as he battled secular humanists on behalf of the unborn. I also knew him as an ethicist with international recognition. He knew Anglicanism (and especially Anglo-Catholics), he knew Catholicism (and especially the struggles of "converts"), and he was the best strategist I knew. A perfect combination for an age-old problem of saints, kings and reformers: how does one get the Vatican's attention?

I understand that I was elected Primate by the bishops of the

Traditional Anglican Communion because they thought I was their best hope to further their dreams of unity with the Holy See. At the meeting of bishops in Coomera, Queensland, Australia, that was held at the time of my investiture as Primate (a meeting that Father Fleming addressed) in November 2003, the bishops unanimously accepted the formula of "seeking unity as an Anglican ecclesial body with the Holy See". This echoed distant Anglican/Roman Catholic conversations such as those held early in the twentieth century in Belgium. It also accepted that the Catholic Church clearly allowed for "corporate reunion" in addition to the more usual pathway of individual reception. When the resolution was put to the vote, the bishops spontaneously rose to their feet and sang that moving Anglican verse known as the Doxology:

> Praise God, from Whom all blessings flow;
> Praise Him, all creatures here below;
> Praise Him above, ye heavenly host;
> Praise Father, Son, and Holy Ghost.

This would not be the last time that this moving verse became an instrument of voting in the Traditional Anglican Communion.

With the backing of the bishops clearly in place, I decided that I would approach each national synod in turn. My own Australian Synod met at the time of my investiture, and powerfully endorsed the bishops' strategy.

But before I met my own people, I wrote at length to the Council for Christian Unity, seeking a meeting and making, among others, the point that the Traditional Anglican Communion was uniquely placed to deepen its unity with the Holy See. I also made the point that, for the first time in the Traditional Anglican Communion's correspondence, I believed there were no doctrinal or moral matters that were of such significance as to form an impediment to full unity. The Council responded that it was not opportune to meet at that time. Undeterred, joined by the then Fathers (later to be consecrated bishops together) Moyer and Chislett, I made a personal pilgrimage to Rome, and prayed in the four great basilicas that the Lord of Unity would find a pathway for us. Providentially, we were introduced to three people: a layman on the Council of the North American College, a theologian from the Congregation for the Doctrine of the Faith, and then with the then bishop for the "Anglican Use" in the United States, Cardinal Law. (The Anglican Use is a provision for Anglican parishes coming into communion with the Catholic Church to retain elements of their Anglican tradition and liturgy.) These men, each in their own way, took our cause to heart and began to open the way for us to deal with the Congregation for the Doctrine of the Faith, which actually receives and assesses applications for corporate reunion. I would return for the funeral of the late Pope, a formal meeting at the Council for Christian Unity, and informal but very intense conversations with people from the CDF. And they took us to the evening hour of prayer for unity in the Church of Saint Mary in Trestevere, packed with young people. We were no longer alone.

Then followed the lunch with Father Fleming, and the clear strategy that emerged.

England, with arguably the strongest cultural anti-Catholicism in the Anglican world, would be next. I called a national meeting in the parish church of Saint Agatha, Portsmouth. This was one of the original Anglo-Catholic churches, built in the slums that surrounded the old naval dockyards. Its founding parish priest, Father Dolling, was forced from the parish when he installed a Requiem altar and reintroduced Masses for the Dead into Anglicanism. This was the church where our bishops would meet four years later and sign the petition to the Holy See, together with the *Catechism of the Catholic Church*, on the altar. As on that later occasion, I was a man of little faith at the start of the meeting, and expected trouble. I must have spoken on our proposal for well over an hour, and with trepidation asked for questions. There were none, and silence reigned, until an elderly priest in the front row struggled to his feet (he had a walking frame) and asked "Archbishop, what about contraception?" I gained several decades of purgatory with my reply, "Father, I do congratulate you for still being interested!" Slightly flushed with guilt, I went on to explain that young clergy and young laity in the Traditional Anglican Communion expressed open admiration for the papal encyclical on contraception, and saw sexual orthodoxy as part of their Christian discipline, in contrast, in many cases, to their parents. So it really is a problem of the older generation. That has indeed been my experience in many countries. And that was the end of the questions. There was no opposition among these people and their clergy.

The next meetings were in Southern Africa. Here, there had been practical tolerance and cooperation between Anglicans and Roman Catholics for generations, and a deliberate avoidance of direct competition. This was also Anglo-Catholic heartland. Sunday High Mass usually begins with a street procession through the township, with incense, cross and many acolytes in red and white. I remember my surprise on a visit some years before, seeing the queue of children after school waiting to make their confession before a Holy Day. The queue came out of the church and down the street! Again, perhaps because of the tolerance, and because Catholic and Anglican bishops had stood side by side in the fight against apartheid, there was a high spirited unanimity for unity.

And then I went to India, to our most populous church. The Traditional Anglican Communion in India had emerged from the refusal of some Anglicans, including bishops and priests as well as people, to be merged into the Churches of North and South India that were formed (more or less by government decree) after independence from Britain. These new pan-Protestant churches compromised Catholic doctrine on Holy Orders and the other sacraments, among other things. So these people were by their own choice following Catholic practice at very considerable cost to themselves. We had been involved in over two hundred court cases, as the new churches claimed parish properties from those whose families had worshipped in them for generations. I could be confident of the faith of the Indian members of the TAC, but I had no clear idea of their experience of Roman Catholicism. I need not have worried. The Archbishop in India, Samuel Prakash (whose father had been Archbishop before him, and whose son is now a priest!) passionately embraced the cause of unity. Passion is the only word. "We are with you in unity with the Holy See, Archbishop, because we have our Christian faith from one of the Apostles himself!" He spoke glowingly of his experience of the ancient and distinctive Indian Christians, and inferred that an Anglican Catholic rite would be a completion of the work of Saint Thomas. Who was I to introduce Australian logic? I would not have thought that this desire of ours for unity was part of the great drama of apostolic history. Perhaps that was another moment of my little faith. India was part of the unity process.

And then back to Africa, for a long stay with the Anglican bishop of Ruvuma, whose brother teaches theology at the National Catholic Seminary of Tanzania, and another affirmation. There were singing and dancing as we celebrated the possibility of a greater unity in the face of a vigorous local Islam. And there was surprise among the clergy that such a thing might be possible.

And so to the USA. The General Synod met in Portland, Maine. Americans are notoriously independent, and American Anglicans have a sense of Roman Catholicism as big and powerful. And uniquely, the Anglican Diaspora in the United States has been prone to splits, animosities, power games and at times an appearance of anarchy. And yet this synod not only joined the endorsements, it did so with gusto. Again, there were no complaints except about the time that it was all taking.

Finally, I went to Canada. This last of the General Synods met in Nova Scotia. Canada is a cradle of the Anglican Diaspora. I spoke longer than usual, perhaps comfortable among old friends. At the end of my remarks, I said, "No Anglican bishop has ever spoken to his people in these words. I am asking you to endorse our plea for unity with the Holy See, a unity accepting the Catholic faith in its fullness, without seeking to negotiate the faith, but to accept it, to do as Jesus demanded of us and to accept the authority he placed amongst us." I expected a vote. Instead there was a standing ovation that went on and on, as I returned to my place and sat down. I was not at all conscious of the ovation being for me. It was an unleashing of the desire for unity that many of these people had held all their lives – not to go alone to the Catholic Church, but to go as a church, in the same way that their ancestors had left it.

I was now confident that the bishops could seek unity, and that the overwhelming majority of the clergy and people of our Communion would come with us. I knew of other Anglicans who had written of "looking behind, and no-one was following". But what to do next? I was hearing reports that the Holy Father was indeed looking to make some formal provision for Anglican groups in the increasing fracturing of the Anglican Communion. Would events overtake us? And leave us behind?

In April 2007, I met with a small group – four bishops, a vicar-general and a layman – at Lincoln in England. We met for three days, and on the final day resolved to draft a letter to the Holy Father personally. We greeted him, and noted that we understood that he was considering a statement on Anglicans. We wanted him to know that our Communion would be meeting in Plenary Session in October 2007, and that if the Holy Spirit willed, the bishops would sign a petition for full, corporate reunion with the Holy See. A single page, with all our hopes on it. We got in two cars and drove to Walsingham, to the greatest of the English shrines of Our Lady. There, we placed the letter on the altar of the Holy House at the Anglican Shrine, lit votive candles, and said the Rosary. Then the letter was taken to the red posting box in the main street, and posted to Rome.

I had decided (again, of little faith) that if the reply came from the Council for Christian Unity, I would cancel the October meeting, as that would be a sign that Rome was not yet ready for a petition. (And perhaps that simply meant that we were not ready to make it.) Likewise, if it came from a secretary of unknown name. But if it came from the Pope's Secretary or the CDF, then I would go ahead with the meeting. The reply came from Archbishop Angelo Amato, Secretary of the CDF, giving us the Pope's warm greetings for our Plenary Meeting, noting that we expected to sign a petition for unity, and asking us to come to Rome after the meeting and report on what had happened. We responded, asking the time and place, and to whom we would report. The reply came back promptly – we would meet at the CDF on the Tuesday following the Plenary meeting, with Father Augustine DiNoia.

I had a time and a place, but not yet a letter to take. There followed several months in which I sat down over and over to draft the document that I would ask the bishops to sign. And over and over the words were not there. This was a time in which I was being driven to speak to the Catholic diocese which I had fled almost forty years before. I had resolved never to speak of those times, but I found that I could not face an appointment with the Holy See without confronting those times. Father Fleming had already written to Cardinal Ratzinger on my behalf when I became Primate, so there was no sense of deception of the Holy See. It was a personal matter of wrong and disorder. A few days before the Plenary meeting, when I was already in England, and deeply upset and hurting, because of the state of the Church, because of the state of Anglicanism, but mostly because of the state of my own unworthiness, I wrote the letter, in one sitting throughout the night.

The bishops meeting began on 1 October 2007, the Feast of the Little Flower, St Thérése of Lisieux, in Saint Agatha's, Portsmouth, England. On the Wednesday, I distributed the letter and gave an hour for everyone to read it in silence. Then I called on each, in order of seniority, to speak. My predecessor, Archbishop Falk, spoke and set the tone of joyous positivity. One after another they spoke, all different, and all positive. At noon, we adjourned for a Requiem Mass for our departed members, celebrated on Father Dolling's original altar. There was the overwhelming sense of completing the work that he and his fellow Anglo-Catholic pioneers had begun. After all the speeches, with no voice against, I asked Bishop Craig Bottrill, a Canadian lawyer, to chair a review of the wording of the letter. Only one word was changed, strengthening the statement on "ex cathedra" papal pronouncements. At four o'clock, I asked all those in favor to stand in their places. All stood, and began to sing Newman's great hymn "Firmly I believe and truly". And then the Doxology, that had echoed at each vote in this five-year process. And then, on a cold English day, for the first time that week, the sun shone through the high stained glass in shafts on the little group, who had voted for something never voted for by Anglican bishops before.

That Friday, I celebrated the votive Mass for the Unity of the Church. After the homily, in copes and mitres, we signed the letter and the *Catechism* with its *Compendium* on the altar. After all had signed, Lay Canon Cheryl Woodman, the Secretary of the College and a tireless worker for the Anglican Diaspora for nearly thirty years, signed a Certificate for the Holy See as witness to the signatures. Only Cheryl and Father Fleming knew of my personal anguish in the months before that moment. It was good that one of these two friends was there.

After Communion, the documents were handed to Bishops Mercer and Wilkinson, who would accompany me to Rome.

I went slowly to Rome by train, dreading rather than looking forward to the meeting. After seventeen years since our first visit, would this be better?

Our welcome could not have been more beautiful. We handed over the letter. Then, noting that there were perhaps already copies of these books here at the CDF, we slid the Catechisms across the table. There was a long silence. Father DiNoia said, "This is a moment of history!" And the first questions asked were about the structure that we hoped might be established. We discussed many things, stressing that there were no "lines in the sand", no conditions. Bishop Mercer explained that we had experienced as Anglicans the lack of authority, we had watched its effect in other Christian groups, and we sought it now in the See of Peter. As the bells of Saint Peter's rang the Angelus, we stood and said the ancient prayer together.

Afterwards, as we walked from the CDF to Saint Peter's Square, Father Augustine ran after us and hugged each of us. He said, "I have just been speaking to the two young theologians who met with us. I said to them that we have a difficult job, because we are priests, and yet do the work of bureaucrats. But I said, perhaps God put us here just to receive the Anglican letter."

That was enough. We went to lunch, but on the way I went into one of those little vestment shops and bought a new mitre. Perhaps, I said to myself, I have a future. On the night of the vote, I had rung Father Fleming and read him the letter. He approved. At lunch in the Vatican, I rang and described the meeting. He asked us how we now felt. Euphoric, we said.

And so we waited. Father DiNoia had drafted a press statement for me to release, saying that our letter was warmly received by the CDF, and that we should not give interviews until the Holy See had responded to our letter. Perhaps, being Anglicans, our silence has been more impressive than our letter. In our waiting, we were finding peace. Meanwhile, there was a great deal of disbelief swirling around us. "They will never get a reply" seemed to sum up the public view.

On 25 July 2008, via the Apostolic Nuncio in Canberra, came the first intimation from the CDF that all was well. I had expected a letter from Father DiNoia, or perhaps a secretary. Instead, it was a letter of considerable personal warmth from the Cardinal Prefect, Cardinal Levada. He noted our meeting of October 2007, and then wrote:

> As the summer months approach, I wish to assure you
> of the serious attention which the Congregation gives to
> the prospect of corporate unity raised in that letter.

That statement in itself was most encouraging. Corporate unity had not yet applied to any ecclesial community derived from the Reformation. "Serious attention" indicated openness by the CDF to this communal process which was at the heart of our proposal.

But the Cardinal gave a further insight.

> As Your Grace is undoubtedly aware, the situation
> within the Anglican Communion in general has become
> markedly more complex during the same period. As soon
> as the Congregation is in a position to respond more
> definitely concerning the proposals you have sent, we
> will inform you.

The linking of our proposal to the turmoil in the Anglican Communion was a clear indication that the CDF was working towards a structure that could embrace a wider Anglican Diaspora than just the Traditional Anglican Communion. The Church of England had voted for women bishops with no provision for Anglo-Catholic conscience, Lambeth had been boycotted by over two hundred bishops, an alternative, evangelical-dominated movement had been established by the rebel bishops, a homosexual marriage of a priest and his partner had been celebrated with immunity in one of London's more famous churches, the Holy See had issued a rebuke of unprecedented sternness, and the Cardinal representing Pope Benedict at the Lambeth Conference had compared the Anglican Communion to a person with both Alzheimer's and Parkinson's Disease – it has lost its memory of its own history, and it had lost contact with its head.

Cardinal Levada concluded his letter with a warm greeting for me "and your brother bishops". So the path was still before us, but the pilgrims were greatly encouraged on the way.

Early in 2009, we received an intimation that the drafting of a proposal was well advanced, and that there was very considerable debate about the proposal within the Catholic Church. Father DiNoia, soon to be promoted to Archbishop and appointed Secretary of the Congregation for Divine Worship, had made an unusual request for prayer in January: "That if it be God's will, those opposed to this matter will not prevail".

On 19 October 2009 I received the information that there would be press conferences in both the Vatican and London to announce an Apostolic Constitution for Corporate Union between Anglican groups and the Catholic Church. Cardinal Levada and Archbishop DiNoia spoke in Rome, the Archbishops of Westminster (Catholic) and Canterbury (Anglican) spoke in London. On the same day, documentation on the proposed Constitution was released to Roman Catholic bishops, and a statement from the CDF was published.

The Constitution itself, designed as an addition to Canon Law, was not ready. But both Forward in Faith in the United Kingdom and the Traditional Anglican Communion Synod for the UK were meeting later that week. I went to England in time to address the National Conference of Forward in Faith. In my address, I noted the symbolism of my reception of Communion that morning at the hands of the international FIF Chairman, Bishop John Broadhurst.

> In those dark days of the early nineties, we in the Traditional Anglican Communion agreed to support you sacramentally, and to be on a common pathway. That has led us to this moment. I pray that you will continue with us.

Again there was a moment of grace, and hesitation seemed to lift, and the standing ovation was not for the Traditional Anglican Communion but an outpouring of hope that a future was being provided for a group that had seemed to have no future. In his closing remarks, Bishop Broadhurst referred to the early nineties, and the widespread hope of English Anglo-Catholics for an arrangement like the Anglican Use in the United States:

> Then, we asked an ecclesial question and received an individual answer. The Traditional Anglican Communion has now asked an ecclesial question, and received an ecclesial answer.

The Apostolic Constitution *Anglicanorum Coetibus*, with accompanying Norms, was published on the 9 November 2009. It closely follows the desires set out in the Petition of the Traditional Anglican Communion signed in Portsmouth over two years before.

At the heart of that Petition was this statement about the purpose of the Traditional Anglican Communion, and the nature of the Anglican patrimony:

- *To identify, reaffirm and consolidate in its community the elements of belief, sacraments, structure and conduct that mark the Church of Christ, which is one throughout the world.*
- *To seek as a body full and visible communion, particularly Eucharistic communion, in Christ, with the Roman Catholic Church, in which it recognises the fullest subsistence of Christ's one Church.*
- *To achieve such communion while maintaining those revered traditions of spirituality, liturgy, discipline and theology that*

constitute the cherished and centuries-old heritage of Anglican communities throughout the world.

The Traditional Anglican Communion bishops went on to make four definite statements of faith:

The Bishops and Vicars-General of this Communion, now meeting in Plenary Session in the Church of Saint Agatha, Portsmouth, England, on the Feast of Theresa of the Child Jesus and in the days following, have reached the following mind which they have asked their Primate and delegates to report to the Holy See:

> 1. We accept the ministry of the Bishop of Rome, the successor of Peter, which is a ministry of teaching and discerning the faith and a "perpetual and visible principle and foundation of unity" and understand this ministry is essential to the Church founded by Jesus Christ. We accept that this ministry, in the words of the late John Paul II in Ut Unum Sint, is to "ensure the unity of all the Churches". We understand his words in the same Letter when he explains to the separated churches that the Bishop of Rome "when circumstances require it, speaks in the name of all the Pastors in communion with him. He can also – under very specific conditions clearly laid down by the First Vatican Council – declare ex cathedra that a certain doctrine belongs to the deposit of faith. By thus bearing witness to the truth, he serves unity". We understand that, as bishops separated from communion with the Bishop of Rome, we are among those for whom Jesus prayed before his death "that they may be completely one", and that we teach and define matters of faith and morals in a way that is, while still under the influence of Divine Grace, of necessity more tenuously connected to the teaching voice of Catholic bishops throughout the world.
>
> 2. We accept that the Church founded by Jesus Christ subsists most perfectly in the churches in communion with

the See of Peter, to whom (after the repeated protestation of his love for Jesus) and to whose successors, our Divine Master gave the duty of feeding the lambs and the sheep of his flock.

3. We accept that the most complete and authentic expression and application of the Catholic faith in this moment of time is found in the *Catechism of the Catholic Church* and its *Compendium*, which we have signed together with this Letter as attesting to the faith we aspire to teach and hold.

4. Driven by these realizations, which we must now in good conscience bring to the attention of the Holy See, we seek a communal and ecclesial way of being Anglican Catholics in communion with the Holy See, at once treasuring the full expression of Catholic faith and treasuring our tradition within which we have come to this moment. We seek the guidance of the Holy See as to the fulfillment of these our desires and those of the churches in which we have been called to serve.

This clearly affirmed the Anglican corporate identity of the petitioners, the acceptance of the Catholic faith – albeit in its most contemporary form, the *Catechism of the Catholic Church*, the teaching authority of the Bishop of Rome, again in its most contemporary form, as sent to the "separated churches" by the late Pope, and the essential agreement on the nature of the Church as a single living organism – the Body of Christ – since the time of Jesus and His apostles.

The Constitution creates a new canonical body in order to foster the unique ecclesial life of Anglican Catholics. In his letter to me of the 16 December 2009, in which he formally responds to the Petition of the TAC (dated the 5 October 2007), Cardinal Levada makes three important points.

He firstly refers to the fact that:

Some time ago you approached this Congregation with

the request that some way might be found to welcome groups of clergy and faithful from the Traditional Anglican Communion into full visible unity with the Catholic Church, in a structure that could offer support and witness to the many evident graces of the Anglican tradition.

Full and visible communion was our stated aim. Anglo-Catholics, no matter what their liturgical splendour and beauty, do not and cannot at the moment celebrate the Mass in either full or visible communion with any other part of the Church.

He then states that "this provision constitutes the definitive response of the Holy See … to your original request". It is now for us to respond, and for others who have indicated similar desires to respond, to the most significant and far ranging offer of reconciliation between Rome and the Anglican world since the fracturing of communion at the Reformation.

The Cardinal concludes with a telling pastoral comment:

In announcing this new provision and in forwarding details to you, I am only too aware of the delicate process of discernment that will no doubt need to be embarked upon by many of our Anglican brothers and sisters, and no less of the many difficult practical issues which will need to be faced.

This is where this story rests as at the beginning of 2010. But ahead of us is a process that is new to the Church, a healing of Reformation hurts, unity for the ecclesial bodies that emerged at that time, and the "support and witness" of the "evident graces" of the Anglican way. As the Constitution says in its remarkable preamble on the nature of the Church:

Since these are gifts properly belonging to the Church of Christ, they are forces impelling towards Catholic unity.

Appendix

The Portsmouth Petition

From the Bishops and Vicars General of the Traditional Anglican Communion, gathered in Plenary Meeting at Portsmouth, England, in the Church of Saint Agatha, to the Sacred Congregation for the Doctrine of the Faith, concerning their desire for unity with the See of Peter.

5 October 2007

Grace and peace in the Name of Jesus Christ, Our Lord and Saviour!

> "A new hope arises that those who rejoice in the name of Christians, but are nevertheless separated from this apostolic see, hearing the voice of the divine Shepherd, may be able to make their way into the one Church of Christ....to seek and to follow that unity which Jesus Christ implored from his Heavenly father with such fervent prayers."

In these words in his *moto proprio*, Superno De Nutu, the Blessed John XXIII, responded to the visit of Archbishop Geoffrey Fisher.

A few years later, in the Sistine Chapel, in March 1966, the next Bishop of Rome, Paul VI, told the next Archbishop of Canterbury, Michael Ramsey, that he should look on his journey as an approach to a home:

As you cross the threshold we want you especially to feel that you are not entering the house of a stranger but that this is your home, here you have a right to be.

The Holy Father warned of the difficulty of the task of bringing about the unity of "the Church of Rome and the Church of Canterbury":

In the field of doctrine and ecclesiastical law, we are still respectively distinct and distant; for now it must be so, for the reverence due to truth and to freedom; until such time as we may merit the supreme grace of true and perfect unity in faith and communion.

The next day, at the Basilica of Saint Paul's Without the Walls, the Holy Father placed his ring on the Archbishop's finger. They had just signed the Joint Declaration that was intended to begin a dialogue that would lead to full communion between Anglicans and the See of Rome. The Pope used the phrases "our dear sister church" and "united but not absorbed'. These phrases inspired Anglicans who yearned for the reuniting of the Anglican Communion with the Holy See. They waited in prayerful optimism for the fulfillment of the work of the *Anglican – Roman Catholic International Commission*. The Lambeth Conference of 1968 powerfully endorsed the approach to the Holy See of the Archbishop and the proposed work of the Commission. The Holy Father noted this acceptance in his homily at the Canonization of the Forty Martyrs of England and Wales in 1970, when he reflected on the nature of the unity that he anticipated:

There will be no seeking to lessen the prestige and usage proper to the Anglican Church.

These words exchanged between Anglican bishops and the Holy See transformed centuries of profound mistrust and unconsummated dreams of unity.

And yet they were set against contemporary Anglican developments that were already separating the Anglicans who most cherished these new hopes from their churches.

The ordination of women to the diaconate and presbyterate, at first in North America, Hong Kong and New Zealand, and in more than half the churches of the Anglican Communion by the mid-1990's, created a crisis of conscience among those who termed themselves Anglican Catholics, and who held the faith of the Catholic Church on matters concerning Holy Order, the primacy of the Eucharist in the life of the Church, and the authority of the Bishop of Rome in teaching with divine authority concerning matters contested in the Church and the world.

The Holy See, in direct and frank communications with the Archbishop of Canterbury, as well as – with increasing finality – in specifically addressing these innovations in its Apostolic Teaching, defined these Anglican innovations as "new and grave" obstacles to unity.

At St. Louis, just thirty years ago at this time, Anglican Catholics tormented in conscience as much by the disintegration of sacramental life in parish and diocese as by the slipping beyond reach of such recent expectations of unity, met and adopted the *Affirmation*. This was a confession of Catholic faith, a determination to maintain the pursuit of unity, and a commitment to create an ecclesial structure sufficient to achieve these desires, while maintaining communion with those churches of the Anglican Communion that remained true to the commitments of only a few years before. It was explicit about unity:

We declare our firm intention to seek and achieve full sacramental communion and visible unity with other Christians who "worship the Trinity in Unity, and Unity in Trinity," and who hold the Catholic and Apostolic Faith in accordance with the foregoing principles.

It was just as explicit in its Eucharistic teaching:

> … the Eucharist as the sacrifice which unites us to the all-sufficient Sacrifice of Christ on the Cross and the Sacrament in which He feeds us with His Body and Blood…

and about the sacramental life of the Church:

> …the Sacraments of Baptism, Confirmation, the Holy Eucharist, Holy Matrimony, Holy Orders, Penance and

Unction of the Sick, as objective and effective signs of
the continued presence and saving activity of Christ our
Lord among His people and as His covenanted means
for conveying His grace.

And it speaks about the nature of the Church itself:

We gather as people called by God to be faithful and
obedient to Him. As the Royal Priestly People of God,
the Church is called to be, in fact, the manifestation of
Christ in and to the world. True religion is revealed to
man by God. We cannot decide what is truth, but rather
(in obedience) ought to receive, accept, cherish, defend
and teach what God has given us. The Church is created
by God, and is beyond the ultimate control of man. The
Church is the Body of Christ at work in the world. She is
the society of the baptised called out from the world: In
it, but not of it. As Christ's faithful Bride, she is different
from the world and must not be influenced by it.

At almost the same time, the Holy See agreed to the creation of
the *Anglican Use*, by which parishes composed of Anglicans reconciled
to the Catholic Church could maintain an Anglican liturgical and
communal existence. It sadly remained only a possibility in parts of
the United States, and did not necessarily allow for the endurance
of Anglican characteristics over time. Then, and again in the 1990s,
large numbers of Anglican clergy joined the Catholic Church
without formal recognition of their Anglican heritage so recently
acknowledged in Papal and Conciliar pronouncements.

Following the Congress of St Louis in 1977, the then Archbishop
of Canterbury rejected the idea that the ecclesial communities (often
small, remote from each other and whose very existence was bitterly
contested by local and national Anglican churches) that emerged
from the determination at St Louis could be considered part of the
Anglican Communion.

In spite of this, the Lambeth Conference in 1998 called for a new
tolerance and understanding of Anglicans separated from Canterbury.

In practice, it is our experience of the Anglican Communion at this time that the acceptance of the ordination of women in particular, and a strong conditionality on the acceptance of Catholic order in general, has made full and organic unity between Canterbury and Rome a remote possibility within our lifetimes, in spite of the ongoing friendliness of Anglican-Roman Catholic relationships.

In 1990, a group of bishops representing churches of this "Anglican Diaspora" met in Victoria, British Columbia, and agreed to a Concordat establishing the Traditional Anglican Communion (TAC). The initial gathering represented churches in Australia, Canada, Guatemala and the United States. The Concordat sought to establish a single College of Bishops of a single ecclesial communion of local and regional churches, expressly denying (in deliberate contrast to contemporary Anglican praxis) that these local churches have authority

> ...to derogate from Holy Scripture, or to determine unilaterally any question of Faith or Order, the authority for determining such residing in the College of Bishops of this Communion acting with such competent advice as may be available to it.

In 1991, leaders of the new Communion were invited to the Pontifical Council for Promoting Christian Unity. Led by Archbishop Louis Falk, who had been elected the founding Primate, and accompanied among others by Father John Hepworth, who has since been elected Primate in succession to him, they met with the late Archbishop Pierre Duprey. At the conclusion of a day-long consultation, in which the desire to achieve unity with the Holy See was clearly expressed, the late Archbishop gave this advice: "You must learn to grow and show that you can grow; you must show us that you can develop good relationships with the local Catholic Church in the places where you both co-exist; and I beg you to not needlessly amplify your episcopate".

Since that time, the TAC has accepted and sought to implement that advice.

A substantial part of the historic Anglican Church of India (consisting of bishops, clergy and people who had refused to join the Churches of North and South India in order to maintain an authentic sacramental life) was the first addition, just after the Concordat was ratified.

The TAC has Provinces, Dioceses, Parishes and Missionary Districts worldwide, and has a presence in Canada, the United States, Puerto Rico, Guatemala, India, Pakistan, Japan, Australia, New Zealand, the Torres Strait, Great Britain, Ireland, several European countries, South Africa (including a substantial part of the Order of Ethiopia – the Church of Umzi Wase Tiyopiya), Zimbabwe, Botswana, Mozambique, Zambia, Kenya, DR Congo Cameroon, El Salvador, Columbia and Argentina.

The Communion exists only where there is a breakdown of sacramental life and order that endangers the spiritual welfare of faithful people. It has a firm policy of waiting until there is a locally expressed need that cannot be met by provisions made for conscience by local Anglican churches. Very few Anglican provinces have made such provision.

Warm and practical relationships have developed at the personal and parochial level in many places. The Servants of the Sacred Cross, a religious institute for women, approved by the Holy See, with both Traditional Anglican and Roman Catholic women members, has grown strongly and spread from North America to Australia. Other Institutes of Dedicated Life, reflecting the traditions of Anglican history, have been founded and grown with Roman Catholic co-operation and encouragement. Our ordinands in some places have been able to complete theological studies at Catholic Universities and theological institutes. Friendships have grown between our bishops and Roman Catholic bishops.

In these growing relationships, we have been sensitive to the fact that formal processes designed to achieve unity between Canterbury and Rome continue to exist, and our presence can be a source of friction between local Anglican and Catholic bishops, particularly where the Anglican bishop has initiated canonical and legal measures against those whose conscience has driven them towards us. This Communion has active Concordats of Communion with Forward in Faith (an ecclesial body whose membership is largely if tenuously within the Anglican Communion) in Britain, North America and Australia, allowing the fullest possible cooperation with those Anglicans whose faith matches our own, but who have managed to maintain an existence within the Anglican Communion. These Concordats are being actively contested in parts of the Anglican Communion, to the further straining of local ecumenical relationships, loyalties and friendships.

There are presently thirty-eight bishops actively holding Episcopal office in this Communion.

Since 1990, this Communion has sought to form its clergy and people in such a way that the College of Bishops could reach a decision to seek the further guidance of the Holy See in the fulfilment of its desire to come as an ecclesial community into communion with the See of Peter, with confidence that they have the support of their clergy and people.

In the past five years, the Diocesan and National Synods of the Communion have discussed and supported this desire of their bishops, often with a longing expressed with moving passion. We acknowledge that this testing of the depth of our support for unity with the Holy See has often attracted media interest, to the embarrassment of our Roman Catholic friends. We grieve for any hurt that our necessarily open processes have caused, at the same time asking for understanding in our desire not to place before the Holy See a proposal unsupported by our clergy and the leaders of our laity.

During that time, we have taken counsel from a number of Roman Catholics, many formerly Anglicans. In the course of that consultation, which was at once informal and rigorous, descriptions of our Communion have been written by our mentors in the context of our quest for unity. One in particular we have been moved to make our own, encapsulating as it does our desire to accept the Catholic faith in all its fullness, while bringing that faith to reality in an ecclesial community faithful to our history and tradition:

Because the Lord has not yet returned in glory, the complete unity and communion of believers for which He prayed has not yet been achieved, but each believer and each church and ecclesial community, recognising the life-changing unity engendered by our shared baptism, is called to make Christian unity a lifelong commitment, just as we are called to spread the Gospel to the whole world.

Recognising that obligation, and with great confidence in the Lord and in the power of the Holy Spirit, a worldwide community of Anglican Christians has united under the name "The Traditional Anglican Communion" for three main purposes:

- To identify, reaffirm and consolidate in its community the elements of belief, sacraments, structure and conduct that mark the Church of Christ, which is one throughout the world.
- To seek as a body full and visible communion, particularly eucharistic communion, in Christ, with the Roman Catholic Church, in which it recognises the fullest subsistence of Christ's one Church.
- To achieve such communion while maintaining those revered traditions of spirituality, liturgy, discipline and theology that constitute the cherished and centuries-old heritage of Anglican communities throughout the world.

The Bishops and Vicars-General of this Communion, now meeting in Plenary Session in the Church of Saint Agatha, Portsmouth, England, on the Feast of Theresa of the Child Jesus and in the days following, have reached the following mind which they have asked their Primate and delegates to report to the Holy See:

1. We accept the ministry of the Bishop of Rome, the successor of Peter, which is a ministry of teaching and discerning the faith and a "perpetual and visible principle and foundation of unity" and understand this ministry is essential to the Church founded by Jesus Christ. We

accept that this ministry, in the words of the late John Paul II in Ut Unum Sint, is to "ensure the unity of all the Churches". We understand his words in the same Letter when he explains to the separated churches that the Bishop of Rome "when circumstances require it, speaks in the name of all the Pastors in communion with him. He can also – under very specific conditions clearly laid down by the First Vatican Council – declare ex cathedra that a certain doctrine belongs to the deposit of faith. By thus bearing witness to the truth, he serves unity". We understand that, as bishops separated from communion with the Bishop of Rome, we are among those for whom Jesus prayed before his death "that they may be completely one", and that we teach and define matters of faith and morals in a way that is, while still under the influence of Divine Grace, of necessity more tenuously connected to the teaching voice of Catholic bishops throughout the world.

2. We accept that the Church founded by Jesus Christ subsists most perfectly in the churches in communion with the See of Peter, to whom (after the repeated protestation of his love for Jesus) and to whose successors, our Divine Master gave the duty of feeding the lambs and the sheep of his flock.

3. We accept that the most complete and authentic expression and application of the Catholic faith in this moment of time is found in the Catechism of the Catholic Church and its Compendium, which we have signed together with this Letter as attesting to the faith we aspire to teach and hold.

4. Driven by these realisations, which we must now in good conscience bring to the attention of the Holy See, we seek a communal and ecclesial way of being Anglican Catholics in communion with the Holy See, at

once treasuring the full expression of Catholic faith and treasuring our tradition within which we have come to this moment. We seek the guidance of the Holy See as to the fulfillment of these our desires and those of the churches in which we have been called to serve.

With profound expressions of regret for the divisions of Christ's Church, and for our own failings that may have deepened and extended those divisions, and with the most affectionate regard for the Holy Father, who at key moments has strengthened us by his concern for our plight, and with great hope in the overshadowing power of the Holy Ghost, who can make pliable what has become rigid, we affix our signatures to this Letter and to the accompanying Catechism in the midst of the Holy Sacrifice and commend our cause to Your Excellencies,

I certify that I have witnessed the signing of this Letter with the Catechism and its Compendium by each of those attending the Plenary Meeting of the College of Bishops of the Traditional Anglican Communion, having also witnessed each of the above bishops and Vicars General vote with unanimity to support the attached resolution taken after a day-long debate on 3rd October 2007.

Lay Canon Cheryl Woodman
Secretary to the College
5th October 2007

INDEX

John Fleming

Convinced by the Truth

John Fleming